SharePoint records management and metadata

Digital archiving in Office 365

Alfred de Weerd

ISBN: 15 19 20 26 87

ISBN-13: 978 15 19 20 26 80

About the author

Alfred de Weerd is Principal IT architect at CGI. He specializes in realizing SharePoint solutions that meet the needs of the users. He has experience with SharePoint records management, knowledge management and information architectures within various government authorities and multinationals since 2007. Alfred studied chemistry, psychology and computer engineering. Most of all, he is a SharePoint user who enjoys showing that a great deal is possible without using customized solutions

About the reviewers

Tom Wight has been active in the field of information technology for ten years now and is currently Senior Advisor Information and Records Management at the Dutch Ministry of VWS (Health, Welfare and Sport). He advises on information issues and is involved with information management at policy level. He fulfils the role of intermediary between the user organization, management, information management and ICT. In addition, he has a group-wide advisory role in the field of information management and information policy.

Stefan Lankester has been active as a Senior SharePoint Consultant at CGI since 2007. As lead developer, he has been involved in projects with governments and in industry. Within CGI Netherlands, he was a member of the SharePoint core team for many years, which aimed to broaden and deepen the knowledge of SharePoint within the organization. He runs courses both at beginner level and advanced level. In recent years, his work has focused on the standard applications of SharePoint and security aspects.

Contents

Preface

Most organizations struggle with records management. They have a vast landscape of unstructured information, which is highly dynamic. Structuring this information is very difficult, due to the high degree of complexity. Implementing and maintaining records management in this environment is both extremely complex and costly. There are two basic ways to deal with this:

- Invest more and more money and have the complexity of your business reflected in your records management system and procedures
- Make bold decisions and simplify, simplify, simplify until you have a workable and cost-effective environment

SharePoint is the perfect tool for the second option, as I am going to demonstrate in this book:

- It supports document management, collaboration and records management, so it is easier to create solutions that both address the records management requirements in day to day use and integrate records management in your processes
- From the user perspective, this means a common user interface and very high usability, SharePoint document-related features, search and metadata capabilities are available in the records management domain as well
- From the information perspective, this means that the same information classification can be used
- From the technical perspective, this means that no additional (very expensive) records management tooling has to be acquired. Although SharePoint can be connected to several pure records management systems, this introduces many complexities

Although records management is an obligatory chapter in many thick SharePoint books, I think this book is special:

- When you read SharePoint books you will notice that they deal with every problem from the perspective of....SharePoint. In this book I take a different approach. Records management and metadata are the starting point. From there on, I demonstrate which of the many features of SharePoint best match the requirements. By following this approach, we will see that many records management requirements are not filled in by using the traditional SharePoint records management features, but by using the rich general SharePoint functionality in new ways
- The methods and standards of records management, such as ISO 15489, are discussed in their relation to SharePoint based records management
- As far as I could find, there is no other text that treats records management on the SharePoint side so thoroughly. It is both much broader and deeper than any other book. Yet the overall size of the book is limited

In practice, I see two problems occurring in SharePoint implementations:

- A strong focus on the technology. A great deal of functionality is created, which sadly remains unused, because the business has different needs. This is often the case when the IT department launches the solution
- A great emphasis on the information aspect. The organization cannot get a grip on the information architecture and the functionality remains abstract. New ideas keep appearing which undermine the work that has been done previously. It eventually turns out that the functionality is hard to implement in SharePoint, and a customized solution is required. This is often the case if the initiative is exclusively launched from the business

An important part of this book is a workable demo for records management, which can used to avoid the problems mentioned. In short cycles, insights from the business are implemented in SharePoint. Because everyone can test the solution in practice, problems and lack of features can quickly be found. Quick configuration allows for an updated version within days. A workable demo is very stimulating, for functionality is quickly growing (not least for the sponsor who funds the project).

The workable demo in this book is also used to analyze issues that may emerge in records management, and to design various alternative possible solutions for SharePoint. The discussion therefore extends far beyond just listing the features of SharePoint records management and step-by-step configuration.

This book is intended for:

- Records managers who are interested in the possibilities of SharePoint
- Analysts who want to align their functional design with the features of SharePoint, so they can avoid designing a system that is very hard to implement
- SharePoint administrators who wish to think more from the perspective of the organization, so they can match the SharePoint records management solution to the real business needs
- SharePoint designers and developers who wish to produce fewer customized solutions and take better advantage of the standard possibilities of SharePoint
- Information managers, architects and others in search of a deep understanding of SharePoint records management or metadata.

The theoretical parts of this book apply to all versions of SharePoint, starting from SharePoint 2010.

The practical examples and the workable demo of this book were created in Office 365 (SharePoint Online) during 2015. They are also applicable to SharePoint 2010 and 2013, without many changes. Major differences compared to SharePoint 2013 are discussed in the text. Since Microsoft does not mention any changes in records management capabilities for SharePoint 2016, I expect this book to be applicable to this version as well.

Chapter 1

Introduction

Records

According to ISO 15489, a record is: "information created, received and maintained as evidence and information by an organization or person, in pursuance of legal obligations or in the transaction of business".

The bottom line is that a record is an important document for the organization, which represents evidence that the organization has fulfilled its legal obligations and has acted in an appropriate manner. Not all documents need to be records. Many documents are important just in their day-to-day use, such as the supporting documents in projects. They do not represent evidence and although they might have a crucial effect on the way people think and act, the real records will probably be the ones in which decisions are proposed or approved. Records may be both physical, such as a paper document, and digital. This book will focus on digital records

Within governments, there is a strong focus on keeping track of transactions, of which the record forms a piece of evidence. Any document that is received, created and sent by the organization is considered to be a record. In the commercial sector, recording actions is less important: records are mostly just important documents, with a commercial value.

In general, keeping only the document itself as a record is not enough. Additional information is required to recreate the context in which the document was created. As a simple example: it makes great difference whether a document is a product of a local working group, or it is approved by the president of the company. Metadata makes clear in this case what the status of the document is. Other common metadata are the name of the author, the owner, date of creation and of last edit, and the document type. Metadata is in fact an essential part of the record. Chapter 8 deals with metadata specifically, but metadata plays an important role throughout this book.

> Records are essential for the company, but the evidential value goes unnoticed until this evidence is actually requested. Therefore, records management may receive little attention in some organizations, especially when there is a strong focus on the primary processes.

The definition of records in ISO 15489 focuses on the evidential value of information for the company. Because digital records are retained in a records management system (or in SharePoint: the records center), the term 'records' is also used as: "the information that is located in the records management system". So there is both an information science-based definition of 'record' therefore as an IT-related description. In this book, the two forms will be used next to one another, the meaning will be clear from the context. In discussions between business and IT, however, make sure you are talking about the same thing. The IT-related meaning of 'record' is shifting to a form where records do not always have to be placed in a records management system. We will deal with this later on and see that this may have a big effect on how you deal with records in SharePoint.

Document management, records management and archiving

A document management system (DMS) enables us create, change and publish a document in a simple and controlled way. It also supports storage and ordering of documents as well as cooperation on documents, applying, for example, version control, search and metadata. SharePoint is such a document management system. In a DMS, the documents are dynamic by nature, with a great deal of changes and consultations.

Records have to be retained for a certain amount of time under controlled conditions. The document management system is too dynamic and too informal for this. This is why documents are 'declared' (SharePoint jargon) records and transferred to a records management system (RMS). See document 2 and record 2 in Figure 1.1. The criterion is that the record needs to have value for the company or has to be able to serve as evidence. When document 2 has gone through various draft versions, for example, the value increases when it has been checked or approved by various people. For the traditional archivist within the government, the criterion for transfer to the RMS is that the case has been completed or that the file has been closed. Of course a document may never comply with this criterion. In this case, the document remains in the DMS throughout its entire lifecycle, see document 1 in Figure 1.1. Finally, a newly arrived document may also immediately be a record according to the criterion. In this case, the lifecycle is the same as that of record 3. The document then immediately ends up in the static phase.

The records management system houses the facilities for retaining and destroying information in line with pre-defined policies. The functionality that a RMS should have is described in standards, such as ReMaNo and DoD 5015.2. Within SharePoint, records centers can be implemented, enabling SharePoint to act as a records management system. Compared to the standards however, it lacks functionality, as a result of which SharePoint is not certified for this standards. This is by design however, and SharePoint does not need to be an inferior RMS. It just does not feature functionality that is overly complex or, it provides functionality in a way that was not foreseen in the standards. We come back to this in the section: *SharePoint records management and certification*.

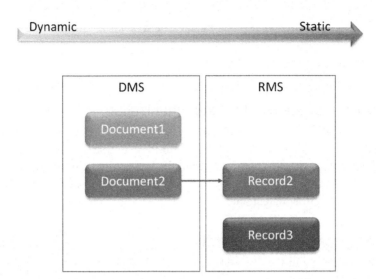

Figure 1.1: Documents and records

Systems that support both document management and records management are also known as enterprise content management systems (ECMS), see Figure 1.2. SharePoint is therefore also an ECMS.

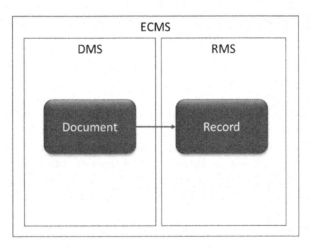

Figure 1.2: Enterprise content management system (ECMS)

At the end of their lifecycle, records may be permanently destroyed, or be transferred to an archive. The aim is not so much to support relevant business functions, but to build historical data that may prove to be useful in the future. An example of this is the National Archive, which retains documents from many government organizations for cultural-historic reasons. Archive documents are basically retained 'for eternity' here. In practice, documents may also be destroyed sooner. Decisions regarding this are taken by the archivist. Due to the very long retention periods, a number of issues play a role here, which are of less importance in records management, such as the physical characteristics of storage (temperature, humidity etc.) and interpretation (codification). To my knowledge, SharePoint is not in use as an archiving system.

Use of records management for the organization

When we defined the term 'record', we already briefly addressed the importance of records. The underlying assumption of this definition is that records always consist of important information. In this chapter, we will further explore the use of records, as this is the foundation for the vision, for the policies and ultimately also for the implementation of records management.

Guaranteeing operational continuity

Within a company, flexibility and stability are the opposite of one another. Both need to be guaranteed in business operations. On the one hand, it is important to be able to adapt swiftly, certainly in the era of the Internet and social media. Both commercial companies and government organizations offer their services on the Internet. Social media have further accelerated the pace of change. On the other hand, there should be a stable foundation, so that the negative consequences of catastrophes or legal procedures may be limited for the company. The discipline of business continuity management (BCM) within the company is responsible for this. Records management contributes to BCM because it enables the organization to give an account of how it acted, and it can demonstrate that the organization complies with laws and regulations. This is why records management is first and foremost a responsibility of the business and not an IT issue.

Accountability

We previously saw that records management deals with the recording of actions. The reason for this is that the organization needs to be able to demonstrate at a later stage how it acted and on the basis of which policy. When, for example, a decision of a government organization has a large negative impact on group of people, the organization may need to demonstrate that it acted with due diligence and could not have done more to foresee the problems or to reduce the consequences.

When organizations are incapable of accounting for their actions, this may result in:

- Claims for damages
- High costs for investigations into the relevant facts of disputes
- Dismissal of the management board
- Reputational damage

For important processes, records management records who has done what, how decisions originated and how they were communicated.

Complying with laws and regulations

Complying with laws and regulations is also a part of operational continuity, although this issue is often addressed separately within organizations, by the legal department. When organizations violate laws or regulations, this may lead to severe sanctions by the government, which directly or indirectly result in:

- Fines
- Limitation of options for the company
- Dismissal of the management board
- Reputational damage

Records management makes it possible for organizations to comply with laws and regulations in the best possible way. Not only because the statutory information is retained in a controlled manner, but also because information is destroyed in in a timely manner in accordance with legal provisions. The latter is important for privacy reasons, for example.

Besides legislation, ISO 15489 also mentions regulations imposed by business or government sectors, voluntary regulations the company intends to comply with and even known expectations of society regarding the acceptable behavior of the organization. In these areas too, companies have a great deal to lose. Business sector organizations may apply financial penalties or r commercial limitations. Reputational damage among customers and the public in general can have a severe impact on an organization as a consequence of reduced credibility. This will have an impact on customers, investors and employees.

Contributions to the cultural heritage

In many government organizations and companies which have been in business for a long time, documents are created which have obtained value over the course of time. The reason for archiving them is not that they still have a direct application within the organization, but that somebody may have an interest in the document in the future, for reasons that are sometimes difficult to foresee in advance. The commissioning of the construction of a new building, for example, may be of interest hundreds of years later when the building has become a monument. Perhaps the building has changed function, and it is interesting to see what the reasons were for designing the building in a specific way. The same criteria apply to companies. They, too, may have an eventful history. It may concern documents that give an impression of how, for example, the company housed people in hiding during the Second World War or how it conquered various crises, which may be important for the corporate culture and the image of the company.

The benefits of destroying information

We saw that there are a number of good reasons to retain documents. A minimalist strategy might therefore be to retain all documents. This is not such a good idea, however:

- More information generally leads to higher costs for storage, hardware and licenses. Furthermore, there are hidden costs that have to do with more complex management and decreased efficiency, because useful documents are hidden among unimportant ones. The latter may lead to a situation where the trust of users in the SharePoint platform as a whole is lost ("it only contains old rubbish"). Decreased findability may lead to a reduction in the quality of decisions.

- Allowing the unrestrained growth of the quantity of documents may lead to technical problems, such as a slow environment or error messages on the size of document libraries and sites.

- The retention of documents also means that they need to be searched and found in the event of a lawsuit. The more information remains, the greater the chance that information surfaces which negatively impacts the lawsuit, and this leads to costs.

Records lifecycle and the records continuum

In order to get more of a grip on the aspects that play a role within records management, two approaches are compared and contrasted in this paragraph: the records lifecycle and the records continuum.

Records lifecycle

The records lifecycle consists of a number of successive stages in the life of a record, which may be presented as a cycle. Figure 1.3 provides an example of such a model. I say 'example' because many similar models exist, with various stages and names. In addition, the models are often drawn as a cycle. This does not make sense to me, for neither permanent retention nor destruction is logically followed by creation. A problem occurring with most of these models is that the steps are not clearly defined. Furthermore, the steps partly occur simultaneously.

Figure 1.3: Records lifecycle

Also linked to the lifecycle is the division into the stages: dynamic, semi-dynamic (or semi-static) and static. In the dynamic stage, the active phase of the process takes place, and all the usual processing actions of documents are performed in a DMS, such as creating, storing, changing, distributing and searching.

After the dynamic stage, the documents are declared records and they enter the semi-dynamic phase. During this stage, the number of actions occurring on the document has sharply decreased. As a rule, these actions are no longer part of the process that took place during the dynamic stage in which the documents originated. Occasionally, new documents are added to cases that are already archived, as a result of the finishing and checking of activities that are basically already completed. Those who are involved in the process normally no longer have direct access to the records then, with access being arranged through the records manager.

After expiry of the retention period, the document may be permanently destroyed or moved to the archive. Thus, it ends up in the static stage. The archival documents are only accessed occasionally, and then usually for an application that does not directly relate to the original objective of the document, such as cultural-historic research. Transfer may occur in the static stage. This involves moving archives to other archives, such as a national archive of the government.

This model has its practical limitations. A semi-dynamic record does not always need to be transferred to an RMS, but may also be declared locally. Microsoft has created SharePoint guidelines on record management,, which can be used to determine whether local declaration or the RMS is the best option. See *Chapter 5, In place records management.*

Records continuum

In the records lifecycle, a sharp distinction is made between the various stages and the systems in which documents and records are stored. Although this is conceptually very clear, matters are more complex in practice. All aspects of records management may apply to the various stages to a greater or lesser extent. In order to do justice to this nuance, the Australian Frank Upward developed the *records continuum theory* in the 1990s. This theory is important for anyone who wants to implement records management with SharePoint. It reflects the innovation in thinking within the world of records management, with which SharePoint ties in. The model is fairly complicated. Because this is a practical book, I present the broad outlines here, without the theoretical particulars.

The central idea in records continuum is that it is too simple to assume a linear lifecycle of records. Indeed, creation, use and storage occur simultaneously or iteratively. Also, the transition from dynamic, via semi-dynamic to static, is not as sharp as indicated in the lifecycle. It happens quite often, for example, that a record needs to be retained as it is, but that changes are nevertheless required. On the other hand, it is sometimes necessary to immediately treat documents that are being worked on as records, for example by recording the context in metadata and keeping track of who changes what in the document.

Features of the records continuum (see also *(1)*):

- It emphasizes the fact that the records management system is intended for business and administrative applications and that it is not intended as a system in itself
- It broadens the boundary of the records management system. The focus extends beyond the confines of DMS, RMS and the final archive. Business targets can only be realized when the components are considered in their cohesion.

- The combination of the two previous points means that the strict line between those who work with documents and those who work with records becomes smaller. The records continuum model makes a case for the integration of records management in business processes and systems.

> The text above indicates that the records continuum does not recognize the various stages of the record lifecycle, instead assuming a simultaneous occurrence of actions and stages. This is a simplification of the theory because I wish to keep this book practical. It would be more appropriate to say that the various stages no longer play a role in the model. The various stages emerge from the model by looking at the model from a different angle. Sue McKemmish (4) compares this with the emergence of the various colors through the diffraction of white light. The various 'dimensions' that are formed this way are not time-related, contrary to the records lifecycle.

The model has four aspects or dimensions (4) (An Xiaomi (3) refers to them as levels) which are crucial for both records management and archiving. The fact that a framework was established which is applicable to both disciplines is considered to be of great added value. These aspects are:

- Create: actions are recorded and reliable evidence is gathered about the actions by creating records. Related or ancillary actions are recorded by linking them to the persons who performed the actions.
- Capture: records of activities in the organization are created as part of the communication in the organization and as part of their place within the business processes. Repeated processes lead to the recording of families of records, which is reflected in the ordering structure. Metadata is organized at this level.
- Organize: an organization-wide process for records management comprising several systems and families of records; this covers all the requirements in terms of documentation (for example: organization, laws and regulations and cultural-historic).
- Pluralize: realizing the collective memory. Information needs are taken care of across the boundaries of the organization. This serves the interests of citizens, governments and businesses.

Being in line with the philosophy of the records continuum, these descriptions are not strict but may be determined from a self-chosen perspective. For example, it is also possible to focus on the maturity of records management systems in the descriptions above, where every next dimension represent a higher level of maturity. See also Frank Upward (2).

The benefits of the records continuum compared to the records lifecycle are best expressed in the differences specified below (for a full list see An Xiomi (3)).

Aspect	Records lifecycle	Records continuum
Origin	Paper environment	Digital environment
Starting points	Focus on (physical) records	Focus on targets
	Product-driven	Process and customer-driven
Status movements of records	Time-based: records have sequential terms, which they go through in succession until they are permanently destroyed or transferred to an archive	Simultaneity: record processes can occur at any point (place/time) in the existence of the record and even before that
Records management process	There are distinct stages with sharp distinctions between document management, records management and archive	Document management, records management and archive are integrated
Role of the records management professional	Passive and reactive	Proactive

In practice, I notice that the department that is responsible for records management is sometimes not well connected with the business. Instead, when it comes to SharePoint, the business is happy to visit the administrator to arrange functionality for document management, collaboration and social communication. As a result, the SharePoint administrator has an advantage over the records managers when it comes to information. SharePoint based processes however are very important for the organization and all the usage scenarios will have to be included in the records management of the organization. The SharePoint administrator and the records manager may both benefit a great deal from seeing each other and discussing how the interests of the business in records management may best be realized with SharePoint.

The records manager and the SharePoint administrator

Larger organizations will appoint one or more records managers. We normally also find several SharePoint administrators in such an organization. The question is often how the responsibilities should be divided. On the one hand, the records managers know the processes, the document flows and the laws and regulations, and they have had thorough training in everything that has to do with records management. On the other hand, records management is actually implemented with SharePoint, where the business is inclined to skip the records managers and do direct business with SharePoint administrators. The records managers also suffer from their image here: only a few decades ago they were primarily the 'custodians'.

It is not keeping but sharing that is hip nowadays. Moreover, demands in terms of daily application, customers and legislation (such as the Dutch act on openness of government, WOB) also require that the information should be easy to find and quickly reproducible. Fortunately, many records managers have long since kept up with developments, partly based on the spread of the records continuum philosophy. They recognized the importance of information technology and the changes involved for their area of work. In this so-called post-custodian discussion (2), it is argued that the professional domain of the records manager is shifting from the actual storage and physical processing of archives towards understanding and managing patterns of data flows and offering context and structure, so that the archives are useful.

What does all this say about the role division between records managers and the SharePoint administrator? First of all, records managers are records management professionals in terms of content. They are used to adopting a proactive approach along with the business in terms of the reflection of processes in documents, liability and laws and regulations. This knowledge is required at all levels of records management and should remain with them. On the other hand, there are social and technological developments with which the SharePoint administrator is more familiar. Microsoft introduced the 'Work like a Network' idea, for example, which ties in with Enterprise Social/Enterprise 2.0. It has an impact on all areas of information management and therefore on records management as well. Based on this, the records manager would have to be responsible for the formal side of records management. The SharePoint administrator is responsible for the implementation of records management, using SharePoint. In addition, the SharePoint administrator advises the records manager on new developments and requirements arising from the business. For the application of new technologies and the development of new and fun features, staff members from the business will much sooner visit the SharePoint administrator than the records manager. In many cases, records management plays a role in social features of SharePoint as well. Yammer, Office Graph and Delve are examples of this.

SharePoint records management and certification

SharePoint 2013 is not certified for DoD 5015.2 or other standards for records management systems, but SharePoint 2007 was (featuring an additional template). Is there a decline? In order to be able to answer this question, we first have to look at what certification for DoD 5015.2 means. In effect, to be certified, an RMS has to comply with the functional requirements laid down in the standards – the same applies to standards such as ReMaNo and MoReq. Whether non-compliance of SharePoint with these standards is a bad thing depends on the usefulness of these requirements. I have my doubts here. DoD 5015.2 is a relatively old standard (the first version dates from 1996). These and other standards seem to have been shaped in a process where increasingly refined measures were prescribed. Because the technological developments of SharePoint make it possible to realize the same results in a more practical way, strict compliance with the requirements is no longer necessary. DoD 5015.2, for example, imposes numerous demands in terms on metadata, as a result of which many metadata fields are required. When end users are forced to fill in all these extra fields they are hindered in their daily work. As a consequence, end users will search for (and find!) ways of escaping the strict rules, which may be as simple as leaving invalid default values in their original value. This undermines the application of metadata and even that of the entire RMS. SharePoint provides some of the most relevant metadata automatically and can be configured to include more metadata automatically. As a consequence, equivalent functionality is established in a more user-friendly way. For more about this, see also Chapter 8, Metadata and taxonomy.

Another example, which also is part other standards, is metadata that refers to other records. So, for 3 relating records, A, B and C, record A has links to records B and C added as metadata. Although the creation of this metadata is easy enough, complexity arises when record C, for example, is removed. Functionality such as the termination of the relationship between the documents is required. The requirements probably date from the era when paper documents were dominant. Applying the same requirements to the letter in a digital record management systems results in complex functionality. The standard functionality of SharePoint (and other RMS systems) makes this superfluous. It is perfectly possible to link the correct documents to one another by sorting, filtering and searching, using relevant metadata such as case IDs, staff member and data. Another option is to use document sets (to be discussed later on). The documents are linked to one another in an apparently looser way, but the same functionality remains available. The advantage of this linking method is that no adjustments will be necessary if one of the documents is removed.

The standards assume a full set of records management functionality. Considerations in terms of user-friendliness and cost-effectiveness barely played a role here. In practice, I notice that businesses can comply with the greater part of their demands with a very limited functionality set. This brings records management back in the focus area of top management, for it is a limited functionality that demonstrably contributes to the objectives of the company, while costing less. When records management becomes too complicated, the high cost of administration and the cumbersome administrative procedures bear no relation to their usefulness. In this case records management will not be a priority to top management. This is indeed a rational decision to make and I see it quite often.

In short: SharePoint is not certified and this is not a problem

References

1. InterPARES: International Research on Permanent Authentic Records in Electronic Systems (InterPARES) 2: Experiential, Interactive and Dynamic Records - APPENDIX 16: Overview of the Records Continuum Concept

2. Frank Upward. Structuring the Records Continuum - Part One: Postcustodial principles and properties. Internet: http://www.infotech.monash.edu.au

3. An Xiomi. An integrated approach to records management. The Information Management Journal, July/August 2003

4. Sue McKemmish: Yesterday, Today and Tomorrow: A Continuum of Responsibility. Proceedings of the Records Management Association of Australia 14th National Convention, 15-17 Sept 1997, RMAA Perth 1997. Internet: http://www.infotech.monash.edu.au

Chapter 2

Implementation of records management

Having discussed the lifecycle of documents and records in the previous sections, in this chapter we will focus on the cycle of activities which leads to the implementation of a records management system. We will mainly focus on the substantive side of the matter here, as well as on aspects that may be traced back to activities in SharePoint. For an overview of activities that specifically focus on (an initial) implementation of records management see *ISO 15489-1 (2)*. This standard delves much more deeply into the more formal organizational and project-based side of records management. Figure 2.1 displays in brown the steps that will be addressed in this chapter. The inner circle features a number of important steps from ISO 15489, where each step is placed with a corresponding subject that is addressed in this chapter. Chapter 3 will subsequently zero in on subjects that mainly deal with requirements analysis and design.

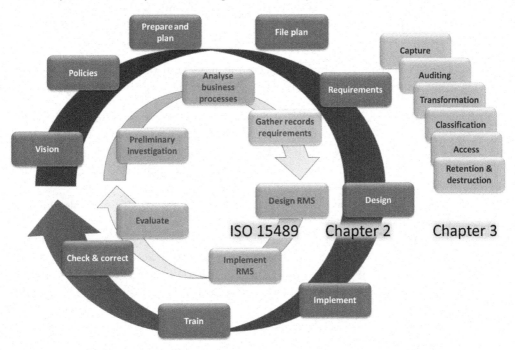

Figure 2.1: Subjects from chapter 2 and 3, related to steps from ISO 15489.

Vision

A proper vision may be set up by specifying the necessity and benefits of records management for the organization (see also the section: *Use of records management for the organization* in this chapter) as well as the risks of faulty records management. In practice, I still often come across situations where the vision is written by the information management department or the IT department. The department is then at a loss what to do: the business does not seem to want to listen to substantive arguments or considers the vision irrelevant. The underlying problem is that the business is not properly involved in the creation of the vision. Ideally, the business itself presents a vision, but this seldom happens. It is also possible to 'pick up' the vision from your own department by interviewing important stakeholders and allowing them to review it. This working method is completed by submitting the vision for formal approval. In the case of records management, this would have to be approved at the highest business level.

Having the vision put together as a responsibility of the information management department may certainly bring benefits. At the company level, the focus of records management is mainly on business continuity management (BCM) and compliancy aspects. So records management is based on the need or obligation to safeguard documents. *Retention, destruction* and *monitoring* are the key words here. The requirements dealing with the *use* of the documents receive far less attention. But if nobody *uses* the documents, there is no point in storing them. As we have seen in the section on the records continuum, safeguarding (input) and using (output) become increasingly mixed.

In brief, a vision is required which connects the input and output of archiving. This vision contains elements such as (see also ICA: Principles of Access to Archives (*1*)):

- The business objectives of the archive, or: why is the archive important to the organization? What direct and indirect profits or cost and risk reductions are realized by the archives and how can the organization further develop them?
- Announcing the existence of the records management systems and the procedures for gaining access
- Proactively offering access via portals and user support with manuals, wikis or forums
- Offering fair and equal access to archives, where there is no systematic exclusion of a user group (this particularly applies to government authorities)
- The positioning of records management in relation to document management in general, knowledge management, case management and e-mail and security policies
- The embedding of records management in governance and business continuity management

In line with the records continuum philosophy, archiving is more than retaining and monitoring records. While it is not necessary to mention the records continuum explicitly, it is good to verify to what extent corporate culture and requirements are in line with this. This information can subsequently be used as a framework on which to base the various segments of the vision.

Policies

Based on the vision, a records management policy may be devised. In view of the strategic importance of records management, the management board is ultimately responsible for maintaining the policy; see also ISO 15489-2 (*3*), 2.3.2. Sections of the policy may include:

- Objective.
- The vision, including the importance of records management for the organization, or a reference to the vision when this is a separate document.
- Establishment of the responsibilities of management – from the executive level down.
- The relation to other policies, such as document management and security.
- The relation to the retention schedule.
- Processes or references to processes. The most important process here is probably the transition from document to record: how can a staff members find out which documents are declared records, what components are automated and what checks are required. See also ISO 15489-2 (*3*), section 2.3.1. Processes may relate to all the elements mentioned in *Chapter 3, Records management processes*.
- Rules or references to rules. Rules may pertain to all the elements mentioned hereafter.

Processes and rules may also be recorded in separate documents, under the responsibility of a records manager. This way, details on processes or rules may be changed while the policy remains the same.

Prepare and plan

Preparation comprises an inventory of the current records management systems, processes, data flows and stakeholders. See also ISO 15489-2 (*3*), section 3.2.3 and Microsoft (*5*). In addition, determining the architecture forms an important element in the planning and preparation of SharePoint as a records management system. This includes:

- The SharePoint environment(s) where records management will be located, through the implementation of SharePoint record centers.
- The various record centers in SharePoint, their topology based on, for example, process, organization, confidentiality or legal requirements (such as *US export controlled*) and the related physical separation in the underlying databases.
- The integration between SharePoint and the other records management systems that have been discovered in the preparation.

There is often a wall between those who do the planning of the content and those who do the technical planning; figuratively as well as literally, because different departments are involved with these tasks. As a result, a mismatch may be created between the requirements of the business and the functionality SharePoint supplies in the field of records management. It is vital to detect such issues as early as possible, so that SharePoint records management may be configured effectively. Conversely, the way in which SharePoint deals with records management may also provide input for the records management discipline itself. I do not plead in favor of making the content subordinate to the technology here. I intend to create a synergy between the two. When implementing records management, there are many choices to make and some choices lead to a better SharePoint implementation than others.

The ISO 15489-2 standard (3) mentions the following steps in design and implementation of a records management system:

- Identify requirements for records management
- Identify strategies to satisfy requirements
- Design record systems

There is, however, a feedback loop between 'design record systems' and 'identify requirements for records management'. Based on my experience, I am in favor of a short feedback loop. So instead of spending months thinking about the requirements, formally approving them, ordering the design team to create a SharePoint design, and then being notified by the design team that there is a mismatch, you should involve the SharePoint administrator or records manager straight away.

Drawing up a retention schedule

The retention schedule is central to records management. The creation of this document requires company-wide input. See *Chapter 3, Retention and destruction*. In this stage, too, it is important to immediately factor in the applicability within the tools to be used, in our case: SharePoint. The question is whether the retention policy can be implemented with SharePoint. If this is not the case, then the options are:

- Applying customized solutions, so that SharePoint is capable of implementing the specified retention policy.
- Simplifying the retention policy, so that it fits within SharePoint. This is not an option when legislation enforces implementation that cannot be realized with SharePoint. In all other cases, the business targets as identified in the vision form the basis for making trade-offs. The question is then whether or not the target is reached if a simpler, more consistent retention policy is specified. Generally speaking, I notice that requirements are often defined independently from the platform. Of course, this ties in perfectly with the idea of the 'ivory tower' of requirements, where a platform is selected and shaped to make it comply with these requirements. This has led to dramatic, complicated, time-consuming and expensive projects in standard packages such as SAP and SharePoint. Certainly

with the emergence of Software as a Service (SaaS), this trend is reversing, and requirements need to be adapted to fit in the platform. SaaS is software that is offered in the Cloud and for which the organization does not need to perform technical management. Microsoft offers Office 365 as a SaaS product and SharePoint Online is part of this. Changing requirements to adapt to the platform is often perfectly possible – the idea that your own company is so unique that it does not fit in a standard package is usually based on an illusion.

- Using a tool that offers additional possibilities in the field of records management. Various tools are available on the market which offer records management functionality, whether or not combined with case management and e-mail handling. A number of them are certified for records management standards. The drawback of every tool is that new technology is introduced, for which additional knowledge needs to be acquired or sourced. New tools involve risks. What if the manufacturing company collapses and support disappears? In addition, tool suppliers often have difficulty adjusting their tool to developments within SharePoint. For example, I was once involved in innovation in a SharePoint platform for a government organization. An argument not to switch to SharePoint 2013 was that the records management tool could not collaborate with SharePoint 2013 and the supplier did not know when this was going to be the case. This happened in the year when SharePoint 2013 had already been released. So if the organization did not want to replace the tool, it would have to wait until the supplier presented an update. In the meantime, however, there were urgent reasons for switching to SharePoint 2013. In any case, tools are not the be-all and end-all. They can only do so much and either customized solutions are required or requirements have to be dropped.

- Choosing a different platform for records management and subsequently creating a connection with SharePoint: These platforms often have the advantage of possessing a proven reputation gained over decades in terms of their stability and functionality with regard to records management. The drawbacks of these platforms are often the high licensing costs as well as the complexity of additional applications, servers and the required expertise. This expertise is scarce and expensive. As is the case with tools, additional certainty is only possible with *state-of-the-art* platform design and management. Another disadvantage of these platforms is that they were designed on the basis of a vision that was still close to paper records management and to a lifecycle where the record is very static. The focus is on *keeping* the record, not on *using* it. Implementation in the direction of the records continuum will therefore be difficult and result in customized solutions

Requirements and design of the SharePoint RMS

Those with experience in system development and implementation are possibly surprised that I did not include the formulation of requirements and the design of the SharePoint environment as two separate, consecutive stages. Traditionally, these two stages were always strictly separated, among others in the so-called Waterfall method. Although modern methods have an iterative character and there is a movement from design to requirements, the emphasis is nevertheless on the separation of the stages. ISO 15489 ties in with this as well, featuring the stages: 'identify requirements for records', 'identify strategies to satisfy requirements' and 'design records system'. The ISO standard however establishes many feedback loops, which indicate that the separation is mainly conceptual. The starting point of this book is that proper implementation in SharePoint can only be realized when, in addition to the design being in line with the requirements, the requirements are matched to the possibilities of SharePoint too.

With this leeway, requirements and possibilities may be aligned with one another. This is also the direction in which practice is moving; the times of enormous and endless bespoke projects are over. The use of standard functionality is the trend these days. This certainly applies to SharePoint, which has gone through major developments since the first, proper version in 2007. It also applies to the new generation of SaaS products that have appeared on the market. Because these products are located in the Cloud, there is a strong emphasis on standard functionality.

The supplier is the technical administrator after all, and does not want to run risks with customized software that is integrated with the platform. The focus is shifting when it comes to applying SaaS products. Where organizations previously thought themselves too unique for existing applications and wanted customized solutions, they now acknowledge that their processes and products are similar to those of sister organizations or competitors. Because (SaaS) software covers all essential processes, this is where the focus lies. Customized solutions for other processes are only opted for when this is strictly necessary. Another reason for formulating the requirements and designing the system in close conjunction is the fact that it is virtually impossible to formulate requirements that are relevant, complete and correct with only pen and paper as tools, especially when the requirements are detailed. This is particularly true for SharePoint, as it offers a new way of working that often deviates substantially from the old way of working. It is therefore impossible for users who are barely familiar with SharePoint to formulate relevant requirements. I often see schedules of requirements that are largely based on the old system, which is naturally familiar to the users. The literal implementation of such sets of requirements creates a solution that transfers many of the drawbacks of this old solution to SharePoint, plus a number of additional problems to do with the introduction of customized solutions, which are needed because SharePoint does not fit in well with the requirements.

Getting users to reflect in a way that fits with SharePoint requires a paradigm shift. Many of the older systems were set up based on a vision that was close to the paper archive. To name an example: in a paper environment, records need to have a physical place. The logic of the placement is essential for retrieval. SharePoint has an advanced full-text search functionality available; metadata makes it possible to find records across various dimensions. It is as if the document is located at an intersection of many corridors that all lead to the document. This makes placement logic and rules far less relevant.

The best way of uniting requirements and the SharePoint design is to make a workable demo during the process. This enables everybody to increase their knowledge of

SharePoint as well as their trust in a solution that is based on SharePoint. In addition, any gaps in the standard possibilities of SharePoint will emerge at this stage. Such a demo also immediately shows any gaps in the requirements, for example, regarding the connection with existing processes and the fleshing out of metadata and taxonomy. This book further develops the workable demo in *Chapter 4*.

Implementation

A major part of the implementation is defining the metadata and converting it to SharePoint content types and fields. See also *Chapter 8, Metadata and taxonomy*. Here, too, only close collaboration between those who are substantively responsible and those who must realize the requirements in SharePoint can lead to the best possible result. An example of this is the potential application of Dublin Core metadata. SharePoint has a content type that implements this standard, yet for a number of fields SharePoint has a better alternative. I created a blogpost about this at AIIM (*4*). This text is also included in *Chapter 8, Dublin Core*.

Maximum standardization is required in order to be able to properly implement metadata and make it usable for sorting, filtering and searching. We need to define a taxonomy for this; again, see *Chapter 8, Metadata and taxonomy*.

Another element of the implementation is determining the procedures and standards. These focus on the interfaces between the daily activities of staff and records management. So:

- Where and when do records management activities need to be performed in the process?
- What needs to be done?
- How does it need to be done?
- By whom does it need to be done?

The 'what' and 'how' questions are primarily determined by laws and regulations and the policies within the organization. The practical implementation is partly determined by the possibilities of SharePoint. In several locations in this book, I specified the drawbacks of customized solutions in SharePoint. A benefit of automation in the field of records management is that users are unburdened. Ideally, they do not even notice that documents are transferred to the record center, if this is not relevant to them. A limited amount of customization may be required in order to achieve this. So there are conflicting requirements in this area which need to be resolved preferably at the level of a policy rule or architectural principle.

Check and correct

Records management will die a slow death if nobody checks whether it is carried out according to the policies and if no correctives measures are taken when required. This applies to virtually all processes for that matter. Geared towards records management in

SharePoint, the following issues are of importance (see also *ISO 15489-2 (3), section 3.2.9):*

- Checking the content of the record center: Have new records appeared where this may be expected? In order to obtain an insight, 'search' or a content search web part (CSWP) may be used in the record center. This does require a great deal of experience. In practice, it will often be necessary to opt for a customized solution or to purchase an app.
- Checking document libraries that dispatch documents or records to the records center: Have the documents or records actually been dispatched? Within the SharePoint library, it is possible to create a file plan report that includes the various content types and displays the relevant retention policy for each content type. Combined with a view that includes the content type of the documents, this may provide an insight. This is a manual solution, however, which will only work if the functional administrators of the document library check their library themselves. The check is easier when it comes to case management. In this event, it is immediately clear that certain cases will remain suspended in a certain status if they are not declared records. The same applies when workflows are used in the approval for dispatch to the records center. In practice, it will often be necessary to opt for a customized solution.

Training

Throughout the entire process, managers and staff members should know *why* they need to do records management, *what* they need to do and *how* they need to do it. The training required for this needs to match the objective, the target group and the organization. Besides classroom training, this may, for instance, take the form of online training, work instructions or quick references. See also *ISO 15489-2, section 6.4.2.* Staff members prefer training that is geared towards their own work, so that they are convinced of the relevance and do not need to make the complicated transition from a general solution to their specific situation. It is not practicable to develop all these specific training courses centrally; the required knowledge for this is usually lacking. A solution is a 'train the trainer' set-up, where, in each department, somebody is trained who subsequently passes on the information to colleagues. The pitfall here is that not every department has somebody who is willing or able to fulfil this role.

In addition, management and staff need to be motivated to participate in records management. This motivation is based on a previously established vision, one that features arguments that are also valid at the level of staff. The latter is often forgotten. Unmotivated staff members will always find ways of circumventing a policy; in SharePoint – and probably outside it as well. This may have major consequences for the organization. At the same time, staff members also need to be informed of what they need to do and they need to be facilitated in achieving this. For staff members, the best motivation still remains that records management should take as little extra time as possible and does not disrupt their other activities. Training is required at various levels to get the most out of the SharePoint environment and to run records management as smoothly as possible.

References

1. International Council on Archives, ICA: Principles of Access to archives. 2012.

2. ISO 15489-1. Information and documentation – records management –part 1: general

3. ISO 15489-2. Information and documentation – records management –part 2: guidelines

4. AIIM Community: SharePoint and Dublin Core. http://community.aiim.org/blogs/alfred-de%20weerd/2014/06/03/sharepoint-and-dublin-core. 2014

5. Microsoft: Plan records management in SharePoint Server 2013. http://technet.microsoft.com/en-us/library/ff363731(v=office.15).aspx

Chapter 3

Records management processes

In the following paragraph we will discuss a number of processes for records management, focusing on their application in SharePoint.

Capture

As part of the daily work process, documents are created, modified by one or more persons and then read. In addition, documents are received that are sent from outside the organization. At some point, the document has to be converted into a record. It is not about the document itself, but also about being able to reproduce the situation:

- Content: how is the text intended? Of course, the document should speak for itself, but it is good to know, for example, for whom the document was intended, and where it was located in the decision-making chain. It makes a difference whether a document is based on a management decision or is a preparatory document by staff, which can later be rejected or refined at management level.
- Context: within which assignment was the document produced, who was involved, what was the input that was processed, and in what period was it written? It makes a difference whether a decision was created on the basis of a document in which important information was involved, or whether such information was not known or could not be known to the writers at that time.

Metadata is used to clarify the content, context and structure of a record. It is possible to use Dublin Core metadata for this, or the application profile for the government or municipalities. In SharePoint, this may be done in several ways, see *Chapter 8, Metadata and taxonomy: Dublin Core*. Another option is the application of ISO 23081 (5), or a metadata profile derived from this.

So records are a reflection of the document in a specific context. For reasons of reliability and integrity, the capture process should guarantee that this reflection is accurate. To clarify, a number of errors that could occur are:

- Incorrect creation or transfer of metadata
- Filing an incorrect version of the document in the records management system, for example because a version is included from the wrong stage of a decision-making process

SharePoint makes it possible to send a document to the records center. This makes it a record by definition in an IT/ technical sense. This is a technical action, which has a number of consequences at the user and company level, such as no longer being able to remove the item. With capture, it is important to record the situation as well as possible, and keeping it available as part of a broader work process. The record is a reflection of this situation.

SharePoint offers several standard workflows in order to safeguard the quality of the capture, such as the standard approval workflow. For a more extensive process-based capture, customized workflows need to be defined. This may be done with SharePoint tools (SharePoint designer, Visual Studio) or existing workflow management tools such as Nintex and K2.

Besides the capture of documents that are created digitally, (also called 'born digital') the capture of physical documents also plays a role in the records management system. This is discussed in *Chapter 3, Records management processes: Scanning*. Capture of e-mails is discussed in *Chapter 5, Workable demo, configuration of SharePoint: Archiving e-mail*.

Auditing

Auditing has both a broader, process-based meaning as well as a more specific meaning for IT systems, including SharePoint. Wikipedia (7) describes auditing as "a systematic and independent examination of data, statements, records, operations and performances (financial or otherwise) of an enterprise for a stated purpose." This definition matches the application in ISO 15489. Within IT systems, auditing refers to recording actions performed within the system, with the aim of establishing that data was not manipulated. This form is also known as 'application security audit', which forms part of IT security auditing.

Process-based auditing

ISO 15489-2 (3) section 5 stipulates that, within records management, auditing needs to be able to demonstrate that:

- the relevant information is indeed treated as records
- this is done in a careful and secure way
- records management is in line with business processes
- specific records management processes are defined and monitored.

Auditing should take place from within the internal organization, and this forms an essential support for the validity of evidence. In addition, an independent organization may conduct audits, which demonstrate that the organization also complies with the external standard. This external auditing may take place on the basis of ISO-15489, but also as part of ISO 9001 (6), section 4.2.4. In addition, the ISO 9001 identifies specific records that are required for the audit of the quality system.

Security auditing in SharePoint

A record should be a reliable reflection of the original document and the related context. This is why they can no longer be adjusted after inclusion in the records management system. To achieve this, access control to the records needs to be enforced, on the basis of a clear access policy. However, in many cases this is not enough. Administrators require modification rights in order to be able to administer the records management system, for example. These rights could also be abused in order to adjust records in an undesirable way, i.e. without authorization from the business. In lawsuits, it is required to prove beyond any doubt that the records could not have been manipulated. An audit log may provide this evidence, such as also identified in ISO 15489-2 (*3*), section 4.3.3. A SharePoint records center offers options for auditing. In the configuration, users may indicate which events need to be audited (adjust, remove etc.). The administrator may then have audit reports generated.

Besides demonstrating the integrity of a record, auditing may also be used to record the context during the dynamic stage. Every adjustment is recorded in the audit log after all. In practice, SharePoint versioning is a much better mechanism for this. Audit logs are rather cryptic, while versions are all readable documents. Auditing is primarily a security mechanism and the application should be carefully considered, as auditing may also be used to record who has consulted a document. This data, combined with other data recorded by auditing, may lead to a 'staff monitoring system', which can trace what a staff member did and when. This may be allowed within the context of securing certain secret documents, but it is certainly not recommended in normal situations.

Transformation of files

It is not always possible or desirable to store documents as records in their original form. In this case, they need to be converted. The most obvious example is paper documents that are digitalized by scanning them. Through conversion, the record changes medium, which may have important consequences where the medium itself is relevant, or when it contains information that is represented differently in the new medium. Other forms of transformation include conversion or transfer of data into a different storage format, as well as the transfer of data and application software to a different platform. An example of such a conversion is converting a Microsoft Word document to a newer format. Migration means that the records end up in a new environment, which may influence their functionality (form and structure). Migration also takes place when an existing application is replaced with a new design. As a result, the chances of damage to the document are higher than with conversion. Indeed, better assessment and tighter control need to take place in the event of migration. The distinction between the two is not always easy to make. For example, converting a Word 2013 document of the .docx format to an open document text (.odt format) is migration rather than conversion, because layout differences may occur. The core element is that there should be a consideration of the risks, and whether they are sufficiently covered during the technical conversion and the conversion process.

Reproduction is a risky operation because information may be permanently lost when the reproduction is not a proper representation of the original. In addition, integrity and authenticity need to be safeguarded. In the reproduction, an original could knowingly or unknowingly be replaced with another. In the Netherlands, the replacement of records requires an explicit decision by the responsible government body. Based on article 26B of the Archive Regulation 2009/2012, the following has to be taken into account:

a) The scope of the replacement process, which includes, in any event, a specification of the organizational units and record categories for which the replacement process applies;

b) The hardware set-up for replacement, the selected settings and the peripherals;

c) As far as applicable: the software and the selected settings;

d) The selection criteria relating to reproduction in color, grayscale or black and white;

e) The way in which the reproduction is created; this includes, in any event, the formats, processing activities, metadata and, insofar as applicable, the choice with regard to reproduction per batch of per item;

f) The monitoring framework for correct and complete representation and error correction;

g) The process of destroying the replaced records;

h) The quality procedures.

The above indicates how seriously the Dutch government takes reproduction because of the potential loss or distortion of information.

Scanning

Scanning is replacing an original paper version (hard copy) with a digital format. From the perspective of IT, this has clear benefits:

- Records are easier to find using full text search and metadata
- Records may be subjected to an automated retention policy
- Digital storage costs less
- In addition, the physical version may be in such a bad condition that digitization is the only way of safeguarding the content.

Document scanning features the following key elements:

- Digitalizing the information on paper
- Adding metadata

Data scanning is part of data capture, which also includes putting structurally different data such as e-mails and XML files into the proper form. The first choice to be made during scanning is whether or not OCR (optical character recognition) should be applied. Applying OCR has the advantage that the text is also present in a digitally usable form, so that full text search may be performed on it. This is not required in all cases: documents that are strongly characterized by their metadata will usually be found with the help of hierarchical navigation or a menu. An example of this is old personnel files, where documents are found with the help of the case ID. Optical character recognition is not entirely accurate. Accuracy depends on the paper, the font type and font size, as well as the variation in font type, font size and contrast. This means that OCR is unable to generate a pure representation of the original. A solution to this is combining OCR with an ordinary scan. 100% pure representation is not necessary in all cases. In most cases, it will be enough if you can demonstrate that integrity and authenticity are safeguarded. In a lawsuit, the court ultimately determines whether the document is accepted.

It is possible to make digital improvements after scanning. For example, a page scanned in the wrong direction can be turned again, and other imperfections may be removed as well, such as dog-ears, staple holes and so on. It is important to remember that the scanned document should still be a reliable reflection of the original. So the improvement should never lead to loss or misinterpretation of information. As an example: it is known that scanning with high contrast results in a beautiful white copy, in which, for example, discolorations of the paper are eliminated. But this setting may also lead to the loss of notes made using a pencil. Visual post-control is therefore very important.

The second essential element of the scanning process is the addition of metadata. Especially when OCR is not applied, metadata is the only reference point via which a document can later be retrieved. Metadata may be added to the document in a number of ways:

- Manually or semi-manually
- Based on a connection with an underlying system
- Based on intelligent recognition

The manual copying of metadata is a labor-intensive option. The benefits are that this can be done with minimal IT facilities and that it often produces high quality. This work is generally outsourced to specialized companies. An intermediate form is one where a single metadata field needs to be filled in, on the basis of which other metadata may be derived.

Here, we create a bridge to the introduction of metadata based on a connection with an underlying system. An example is the entry or automatic recognition of a personnel number, after which the connection with a personnel registration system is created. From this system, the remaining fields are filled in, such as the name and date of birth of the person.

An interesting development is mobile data capture, where mobile phones are used to scan documents. This is the opposite development from isolated scanners to scanning lanes with a very high volume. The work is no longer performed by an efficient, centralized solution, but it is performed de-centrally, where many users perform a small part of the job with their mobile devices.

This also means that process flows will run differently. Scanning is done closer to the place where the document is created and closer to the (primary) process. Laws and regulations require that data capture of records should be carried out in a controlled process, where authenticity and integrity should be safeguarded. Because these requirements will remain a given, it is self-evident that mobile data capture will develop along those lines (*8*).

Ordering and accessibility

Accessibility of an archive is about the extent to which various user groups can find relevant data. Proper accessibility is achieved by ordering and searchability. Both are supported by metadata to a large degree.

In order to make an archive accessible, first of all, its existence and location must be known. Within the organization, various user groups often speak about 'the' archive, although several archives are active in several systems throughout the organization. These staff members do have a vague idea that 'their' archive does not contain all the records, but nobody has an overview. This diversity is the result of the fact that some systems, for example in the field of HR, have their own archive that is tailored to the process. Records are stored in the business application where they are created. There is little use in forcing these archives into a general RMS, as this would hinder work processes and create security risks.

Ordering

Correct ordering is the basis of proper accessibility of records. It should be clear and logical. The problem with any ordering is that it may be disputed. In projects, for example, it is easy to see when somebody has made a 'logical' classification for the project documents in a file system, which then proves impossible for others to follow. The result is that similar documents end up in various folders and that various documents end up in the same folder.

A good ordering structure can be created by having it match the classification of the file plan within the records management system. This may be based on the organizational hierarchy, functions or processes, and will probably be a combination of these elements. A classification that only assumes the organizational hierarchy is vulnerable, because this may change fairly quickly. Functions and processes are more stable. As early as 1881, Muller and Fruin wrote a treatise on ordering in their book *Handleiding voor het Ordenen en Beschrijven van Archieven [Manual for Ordering and Describing Archives]*. The key question was whether there are general principles that can be applied to archives, or whether every archive requires its own ordering. In addition, the writers established various ordering principles. A problem here is that the ordering principles partly exclude each other, and that an ordering that is useful to the records manager may not be useful to the users.

Ordering will be hierarchical in record systems of a substantial size. SharePoint offers standard options for implementing the various levels of aggregation; for example: file, series and sub-archive. This ordering results from the tasks and processes of an organization.

Metadata

Within electronic records management systems (EMRS) logical ordering can be realized using metadata, solving the problems described in the previous paragraph. Searching, sorting and automating operations can all be based on metadata. In fact, metadata fields form a multidimensional space. Depending on the desired application, it is possible to provide a relevant cross-section of this space. If this sounds a little complicated, this example may help: let's assume you want to order a book on both the author name and the subject. In a physical library, you have to choose either of the two. Metadata allows for searching and sorting both on author name and subject at the same time. A few more examples will give you an idea of the importance of metadata:

- The preservation of the internal cohesion of documents created in a work process is not only of importance for the interpretation of the documents, it also contributes to the authenticity and reconstruction of the business activity of which they are the result. The cohesion may be recorded in a case number, for example. The order of the documents in a case must be traceable. This is necessary in order to be able to reconstruct the business process. Metadata like this is easily supplied in SharePoint; this also the case for the various ordering levels.
- By using metadata fields, it is possible to create overviews in which items are grouped, sorted or filtered. This is a very important feature which is known to many people, but underestimated. The same information may be displayed in multiple ways, supporting the tasks at hand. A little consideration is required when applying these views. For example, a view could mask the cohesion in records, if relevant records were left out.

Chapter 8, Metadata and taxonomy will focus on metadata and its applications in much more detail.

Management

Besides findability, manageability is an important criterion for good ordering. As records are more related (for example, originating from the same department, process, sub-department or sub-process) their attributes will be more similar as well. This is often translated into management related configuration such as access rights, audit settings, and the underlying database in which the records are stored. These databases may subsequently have their own back-up regime, in line with their own content. Requirements in the field of manageability may provide input for the creation of a practical classification.

Within the SharePoint environment, various record centers may be created which function as archives. At a lower level, various document libraries may be set up in which, in turn, folders may be created. In these folders, records may be created at various hierarchical levels. Here, too, the features of SharePoint as a platform should be included for ideal implementation. It is sensible here to distinguish between logical and physical ordering. The user organization only requires knowledge of the logical ordering. This prevents the popping up of technical SharePoint aspects in discussions on ordering. By creating a proper translation from logical to physical ordering in SharePoint, clarity will be preserved for the end user and the benefits of the SharePoint platform will be used in the best possible way. A few examples of situations in which it is useful to have the physical ordering deviate from the logical ordering:

- When the highest level of ordering includes various volumes of records that differ from each other in terms of content, but do share many management features within SharePoint records management, it is useful to include all records in the same records center. The settings will then not need to be synchronized between the two records centers (which is not a standard functionality).
- If the volume is very large, it may be necessary to split them within various records centers in SharePoint.
- SharePoint records centers use rules to automatically send documents to the right location within the records center. As the hierarchy becomes more complex, the risk of errors in the rules increases. In a records center with many millions of documents, errors may lead to a great deal of work during retrieval and relocation. A flat hierarchy is to be preferred in SharePoint. However, this does not have to be perceptible to users.

Retention and destruction

The retention schedule is a list of important document (types) that will be treated as records and, on the basis of this, will be destroyed or transferred to an archive. This destruction or archiving is linked to terms that are specific to each document type. Retention schedules may also be called 'records schedule' or 'file plan'.

A retention schedule forms a good and formal basis for implementation in SharePoint. So the person in charge of the functional maintenance of the records center does not determine the retention periods. They cannot be changed on an ad hoc basis either, not even at the request of the business. First of all, the formal route should be taken and the change should be implemented in the retention schedule. The standard check by an auditor includes a comparison between the selection list and the terms that are actually used in SharePoint; they should always be identical.

In practice, the responsibility for classifying documents as records and determining retention and destruction times is delegated to the business units. They have specific knowledge of the importance of documents for business continuity as well as knowledge of laws and regulations. As a consultant or SharePoint administrator of a small business, you may end up in a role with the responsibilities and tasks typical of a records manager. In this case, it is important to realize that the business is always responsible for determining the retention and destruction periods. ISO 15489 provides instructions to determine which are the relevant records that match the targets of records management as set out at the beginning of this chapter. See ISO 15489-1 (*2*), section 9.2. The records manager needs to provide useful categories of documents, which may be easily traced back to the processes in which they play a role, and about which agreement was reached with the various departments. A rough, implementable scheme has much more value than a weighty tome that nobody reads. It is then up to the SharePoint administrator to convert the document types into content types in which the relevant metadata is processed. The administrator will subsequently have to implement a manageable records center, or outsource this.

A records manager knows the processes in the businesses, the role that documents play in them as well as the laws and regulations. Based on this, the records manager may provide various business units with advice on the retention terms. However, this requires highly specialist knowledge, and as a SharePoint administrator you should not allow yourself to be pushed into this role.

Retention periods are traditionally determined by balancing the potential use of retaining a record against the costs involved. This consideration is still justified, although storage costs have declined drastically. An increase in the number of records also results in a lower accessibility and transparency of the archive, and it results in a greater management burden. Records may simply be destroyed because the period within which they have value has expired. The request for destruction may also be imposed by laws and regulations. The Dutch Personal Data Protection Act stipulates that personal data may only be retained for a specific, defined objective. This may mean that certain personal records should be destroyed within two years after an employee has left the company. The requirements for removal are a great deal more stringent in this case: the data must no longer be reproducible in any way whatsoever. This also means that all back-ups should be deleted and, in some cases, references should be removed. In practice, it is very difficult to comply with this. Archival legislation and privacy legislation are fundamentally in conflict with each other: archival legislation stipulates retention and privacy legislation stipulates destruction. When conflicting requirements arise, archival legislation takes precedence over the Personal Data Protection Act (*9*) in the Netherlands. A possible solution to resolve the conflict is arguing that there is a new reason for the retention of personal data – for example cultural / historic research. The personal data is relevant then and no longer needs to be deleted. Viewed from this perspective, the contradiction between the various types of legislation is not that problematic.

A retention schedule consists of at least the following elements:

- Description: a description of the features of a document group (document type), in order to be able to distinguish it from other document groups
- Retention and/or destruction period(s) and actions. Besides the retention period, the location of the documents and the manner of destruction are also recorded. Examples of this are automatic destruction or starting a workflow in which approval for destruction is requested.
- The starting point for the retention or destruction period. For example date created/received, last adjustment or a process-specific trigger. Examples of the latter are the signing date of a contract, end of the tax year, etc.
- Rationale: why is the retention/destruction period defined as such? If the rationale is not recorded, then this may give rise to debate later.

Creating a retention schedule

Most large organizations have a department that is involved in creating retention schedules in accordance with their own methods. In smaller companies or in companies where records never received serious attention, the method described here may be a starting point.

Retention schedules may be created on the basis of document type, function or process. An organizational hierarchy revolves around various departments that each have their own manager; a function relates to a part of the organization (such as performing resource management). In practice, the function is often closely linked to a department, but it may also relate to several departments. A process may include several functions/organizational units, but it may also be entirely located within a function or department. Retention schedules based on document types consist of a list of all types of documents in the organization. The various documents are grouped according to type. Such a classification is stable and simple, but lacks relationship with the business. Classifications based on the organizational hierarchy or function follow the structure of the organization or the type of work that is carried out. Structures in organizations are always sensitive to reorganization and the accompanying changes. A classification based on function is considered to be more stable, although businesses have had to change increasingly rapidly and fundamentally over the past decades.

Similar items (document types, functions or processes) may be combined across the various business units, or they may be separated for each business unit. Both methods have their drawbacks and advantages. When a specific item is searched, it may be helpful to have a hierarchical classification in which the first level is the main process or the department, for example. Within a SharePoint record center, there is also the issue that document libraries should not become unmanageably large. The maximum number of items in a view for SharePoint Online (Enterprise) is 5,000 items at present. On the other hand, smart views may be created within a document library, which facilitate the creation of relevant cross-sections for the documents present. As a rule of thumb, views should never contain more than 100 items, and preferably fewer than 20.

The following is a basic working method for arriving at a process-based retention schedule (1):

- Create an inventory for the main processes, which consist of various functions or departments. See also ISO 15489-1 (2), section 8.4b, ISO 15489-2 (3), section 4.2.2.2. It is also possible to start with an inventory of the main processes for each function or department, for processes that take place entirely within such a unit.
- Create an inventory for sub-processes for each main process. See also ISO 15489-1 (2), section 8.4b, ISO 15489-2 (3), section 4.2.2.2.
- Determine the importance for each sub-process and identify requirements arising from laws and regulations, as well as the need for evidence. Statutory tasks for governments, for example, are listed in decrees, see also ISO 15489-1 (2), section 8.4c.
- Determine what records are related to the previous point.
- Determine the retention period for each process or for each document type as well as the event that marks the beginning of the term (for example: contract drawn up, signed at local level, signed by the management board, signed by the client). Determine what should happen with the documents after the retention period.
- Determine the retention period of documents that are not records and what should happen with them after the retention term. This may look similar to the previous point, but the focus is now on the destruction of documents that have lost their value after a certain period.
- For the Dutch government, the selection list is formally established and published in the Dutch Government Gazette.

Set up a main structure for ordering by standardizing the list at as high a level as possible. This avoids a situation where every department invents its own set of document types for processes that you actually want to streamline as much as possible at record level, such as project management. Creating a structure for ordering was the final step taken here, but it is probably more efficient to standardize after the first processes, and to establish best practices accordingly with which subsequent processes should comply. Not only does this create a recognizable structure and you have an influence on the desired detail level this way, it also provides an important reference point for implementation in SharePoint. Here, too, the functional requirements come first, but a workable system can only be created by already factoring in implementation during the process. Standardization offers the possibility of basing similar document types on a shared content type in SharePoint. As a result, the records management solution becomes much simpler as well as easier to maintain.

Microsoft makes a template available on Technet for a file plan (4) which is document-based. Although this may serve as a basis for smaller companies that start with archiving activities, for example because Office 365 makes this easily accessible for them, most companies will use their own schemes.

References

1. Creating a Process-Focused Retention Schedule. Tina Torres. The Information Management Journal, September/October 2006

2. ISO 15489-1. Information and documentation – records management –part 1: general

3. ISO 15489-2. Information and documentation – records management –part 2: guidelines

4. Microsoft. Create a file plan to manage records in SharePoint 2013. https://technet.microsoft.com/en-us/library/cc261708(v=office.15).aspx

5. ISO 23081: Information and documentation - Records management processes - Metadata for records

6. ISO 9001:2008: Quality Management

7. Wikipedia: Audit. http://en.wikipedia.org/wiki/Audit

8. Nota van toelichting Archiefbesluit 1995 [Explanatory memorandum archiving decision 1995]

9. Erfgoedinspectie. Sporen nalaten of uitwissen? Het bewaren van persoonsgegevens [Heritage inspection. Leaving or erasing traces? Retaining personal data] http://www.erfgoedinspectie.nl/uploads/publications/sporen_nalaten_of_uitwi ssen.pdf

Chapter 4

Workable demo: design

Based on the foregoing, we are now going to implement records management with SharePoint. From the perspective of SharePoint, there is the basic classification of records management by means of a records center and one by means of 'in-place' records management. Because of the implementation of records management in SharePoint, combining the two forms in a shared solution is not ideal. Manual steps are required, or a workflow needs to be developed that puts the various steps in a sequence. Neither course of action is insurmountable and, thinking of the records continuum, it may certainly be desirable in some situations to create a combination. In the example discussed in this chapter, we will not do so and we opt for an alternative solution.

Quite a few examples of the configuration of records management may be found online, but the elaboration we will carry out together differs on a number of important points:

- We will not only look at the 'what' and the 'how' of the configuration, but first and foremost at the 'why' and 'when' of records management. Microsoft information, blog articles and books indicate which options you can implement, but frequently they do not make it clear *WHY* you should choose a specific option. This book tries to fill this gap, with due respect for everything that smart, technical people have invented. When you know in what way the requirements of records management may be translated to SharePoint, the actual implementation will no longer be that difficult.
- The example describes the entire solution. It is a simplified example, of course, but it is workable. Examples often only focus on the configuration of the records center, as a result of which the relationship with other aspects remains unclear. Starting from the idea of the records continuum, we know that it is very important not to describe records in isolation.

The result is a workable demo. You can show it to stakeholders and discuss the benefits and drawbacks. Such a workable demo often causes surprise along the lines of: "You've come a long way" and "I didn't know all this was possible". It also immediately triggers responses such as: "Very nice, but sometimes I receive no less than 100 documents, and I need to be able to filter out the right ones". These are wishes that need to be formalized in requirements at a later stage. It helps if you can immediately show how sorting and filtering works in SharePoint. Users will then think in the right direction more quickly, rather than literally translating their current system to SharePoint, which often leads to many customizations. The actual power of standard SharePoint functionality will then remain under-utilized because the solution does not match the SharePoint philosophy. Indeed: I often notice that years later the benefits begin to dawn on people after all, and that a new process is required to translate the customization to standard SharePoint functionality.

A workable demo is a good working method when many stakeholders are involved who still have little knowledge of SharePoint. There is absolutely no use in blindly having users create requirements, hoping that they will later be easily translatable to SharePoint. These processes take a very long time and the result is barely usable. The chances are high that the process remains suspended at the halfway point because other issues have been given a higher priority in the meantime. Moreover, the requirements are often not specifically described and complex issues are not fully developed.

A workable demo can be created more quickly, as a result of which there will be a sense of success. At the same time, it becomes clear that a great deal still needs to happen to ultimately shape the solution. In a workable demo it becomes apparent that 80 per cent of the key requirements can be implemented fairly easily. It is the remaining 20 per cent that leads to a great deal of work and complexity. In the rest of this chapter and in the next chapter, we will create a workable demo for the fictitious company A-works.

Requirements for the records management solution

Every IT solution needs requirements. This is no different for a records management solution. Creating requirements for a records management solution is particularly difficult, because they originate from the entire business and there are many stakeholders, combined with the fact that a number of matters need to be recorded at the detail level. So records managements should not be tackled as an IT project. Implementation with SharePoint is just the final step.

Case

We have now arrived at the description of the fictional company A-works with a records management challenge. Although the case is fictional, elements of what I have come across with customers have been worked into the case and I am pretty sure you will recognize these factors in your organization.

A-works is a company that specializes in performing maintenance work on complex industrial installations. The company has a great number of vans that engineers use to drive to clients. Every type of activity requires its own tools and materials, and this is why there are various vans for working on chemical installations, biochemical installations and electrical installations respectively. In the past, engineers would sometimes use outdated manuals from the vans, as a result of which their work did not comply with the latest standards. This is why all vans are now equipped with a laptop with Wi-Fi. Engineers are supposed to download the latest version of the manuals from the knowledge management system.

Requirements

The following requirements have been established for the records management solution of A-works (the list of requirements for your workable demo might be more extensive, of course):

1. Manuals that describe formal procedures based on laws or regulations have to be stored as records, retained for 10 years and subsequently destroyed.

2. Manuals relating to biochemical installations are to be retained for 15 years and subsequently destroyed.

3. Manuals are created through cooperation in SharePoint team sites, by experts (persons who used to be engineers and who subsequently also obtained knowledge of, among others, laws and regulations)

4. After formal approval, they are included in the knowledge management system of A-works.

5. Only one version of every manual is active in the knowledge management system.

6. Manuals in the knowledge management system can no longer be changed. Every time a change is required, a new manual is formally created to which requirements 3 and 4 apply.

7. Only staff of the legal affairs department should be able to access versions of the records that are no longer in use in the field.

8. Staff at the legal affairs department should be able to find records on the basis of text searching and it should be possible to sort and filter the records.

Requirements 1 and 2 form an informal retention schedule. When formalized we arrive at the following retention schedule:

Manual

Description	**A manual formally records what laws and regulations apply to the work and how this application should be**

Terms	Immediately after approval: retention (10 years)
	Immediately after completion of the new version: retention (10 years)
	After expiry of the retention term: destruction
Rationale	For a period of up to 10 years after the engineering on an installation has been finished, laws and regulations may lead to an investigation in which it should be demonstrated that the work done is compliant with laws and regulations

Biochemical manual

Description	**A (biochemical) department formally records what laws and regulations apply to the work and how this application should be implemented (work instruction)**
Terms	Immediately after approval: retention (15 years)
	Immediately after completion of the new version: retention (15 years)
	After expiry of the retention term: destruction
Rationale	For a period of up to 15 years after the engineering on an installation has been finished, laws and regulations may lead to an investigation in which it should be demonstrated that the work done is compliant with laws and regulations

The design of the solution

We start with the design of the records management solution. I purposely selected the requirements in such a way that they do not only overlap with a records center, but that the larger part of the lifecycle is covered by the solution as well. In fact, the solution already fits in closely with the records continuum.

Even with a short list of requirements, various possible solutions may be conceived, each with its own benefits and drawbacks. It is not that one solution is correct and the others are wrong. The trick is to find the solution with the most advantages and the least disadvantages. This requires a weighting. Without being overly formal – this is not a chapter about architecture – we allow ourselves to be assisted by the following principles here (see my blog (1) for my vision of the importance of principles):

- P1: the interest of the company (business continuity, security) comes first
- P2: ease of use for engineers is optimized
- P3: only SharePoint standard functionality is used

Principle P2 may seem somewhat unfair to the legal experts. However, the underlying principle is the idea that ease of use for people who often use the solution overrides that of people who occasionally use the solution. In addition, in this case engineers require the manual for the primary process and they need to be able to use it via a Wi-Fi connection. It is inconvenient if many actions are required to arrive at the correct manual.

Principle P3 is based on the benefits offered by the use of standard functionality compared to customizations. See also (2). These benefits do not only apply to SharePoint, but to all other commercial off-the-shelf (COTS) products as well.

The first proposal is to use three separate sites in the lifecycle of a manual:

- A team site for cooperation of experts on new manuals or adjustments of the existing ones.
- The knowledge library of A-works for giving engineers access to the manuals in a proper and user-friendly way
- A records center for permanently securing the manuals for the company and for providing legal experts with access

In the team site, the draft manual is a document. Eventually, after it has been sent to the records center, it is a record. In the intermediate stage of the knowledge library, the manual could also be an ordinary document, or an in-place record. In-place records are not located in the records center, but in an ordinary document library.

Requirement E6 stipulates that a new manual should be issued after every adjustment, which means that no changes should be made to existing versions. In-place records support this fact, because they cannot be changed. A standard document library in SharePoint also offers the possibility of countering the alteration of documents by only assigning modification rights to administrators of the knowledge library. Now we arrive at an important point in the design: the implementation of SharePoint is going to play a role. In order to facilitate the relocation of documents and records and to prevent them from accidentally being moved to a wrong location, they can be relocated with a 'send to' mechanism in SharePoint. This allows the document to be copied or relocated. However, the relocation of records cannot be done manually. See also the box below.

> The SharePoint system blocks in-place records, as a result of which they can no longer be manually altered, removed or relocated. They may still be copied. The system itself can relocate records, by unblocking first.

Three different options are possible:

1. Relocate the record by means of copying and then manually remove the remaining version. This feels laborious. In addition, a strong principle in enterprise content management (ECM) stipulates that documents should not be copied but that references should be used.

2. Relocate the record automatically with send to. This should happen when a new version is introduced in the knowledge library. Yet this requires a customized workflow, which violates principle P3. This is an ideal solution from a user perspective (P2) and from a security perspective (P1). When large quantities of manuals need to be sent every day, customization is the preferred choice. Yet this is not the case with A-Works, where it involves several manuals a week on average.

3. Use an ordinary document library, in which the option of in-place records management is not activated. This solution seems less safe than solution 1. In practice, this is not a problem, because authorizations take over the role of records. Only the administrator is allowed to remove documents. In SharePoint this is almost impossible to do by accident. And if it happened anyway, there is always the recycle bin, see (3).

This leads to the following design choice: an ordinary document library is used for manuals that are still used by engineers (E5, E6). Upon discontinuation of use, the manuals are transferred to the records center (E1, E2, E8).

The first draft of the design is shown in Figure 4.1. Documents are created and modified by experts in the team site. This stage is highly dynamic, because the manual may change every day. After formal approval, the manual is transferred to the knowledge library. Here, the manual is frequently used by engineers and it can only be read. Finally, the manual is transferred to the records center. The manual will only be consulted in exceptional cases here. Figure 4.1 is represented as a lifecycle model, in which every step is neatly followed by a next step. The reality is slightly more complicated: while engineers are using the final version of a manual, experts are already working on the next version.

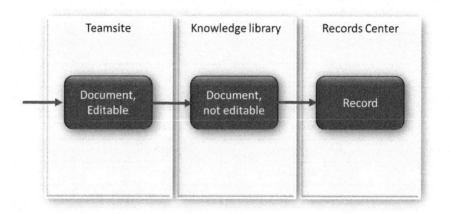

Figure 4.1: The three stages of the lifecycle of a manual.

Content type: ACTH Manual

Site Columns

Column	Type		
Equipment	Choice		

	Property	Value	
	Column name	Equipment	
	New Group	A-works	
	Description	Required equipment for operation procedure	
	Display choices using	Checkboxes (allow multiple selections)	
	Allowed Values	Multimeter	
	Default value	<blank>	

Column	Type		
Installation	Choice		

	Property	Value	
	Column name	Installation	
	Existing group	A-works	

Description	Installation type
Display choices using	Radio buttons
Allowed Values	Electrical
Default value	Medical

Column	Type	
Engineer	Choice	
	Property	**Value**
	Column name	Equipment
	Existing Group	A-works
	Description	Required engineers
	Display choices using	Checkboxes (allow multiple selections)
	Allowed Values	Construction engineer
		Electro-technical engineer
		Safety engineer
		High pressure specialist
	Default value	\<blank\>

Table 4.1: Values for Site columns of content type Installation manual

Retention policy

1. 3 years after creation: remove old work versions

2. Immediately after approval: retention (10 years)

3. After expiry of the retention term: destruction

The destruction of the work versions after 3 years is not strictly necessary from the perspective of records management. The work versions are created in the meantime as a result of the practical process; this includes, for example, interim storing to make sure not all the work is lost in the event of a computer crash. They are not relevant to records management, but from the broader viewpoint of information management, you want to remove these work versions over the course of time. Multinationals often do this with all their documents, because the quantity of old document may become very large. A-works also uses this as a standard rule that should be added to all retention policies.

Content type: ACTH Biochemical Manual

Site Columns

Column	Type		
Equipment	Choice		
	Property	**Value**	
	Column name	Equipment	
	Existing Group	A-works	
	Description	Required equipment for operation procedure	
	Display choices using	Checkboxes (allow multiple selections)	
	Allowed Values	Multimeter	
		Cable puller	
		Stud finder	
	Default value	<blank>	

Column	Type		
Installation	Choice		
	Property	**Value**	
	Column name	Installation	
	Existing group	A-works	
	Description	Installation type	
	Display choices using	Radio buttons	
	Allowed Values	Electrical	
		Biochemical	
		Medical	
	Default value	Biochemical	

Column	Type		
Engineer	Choice		

	Property	Value	
	Column name	Equipment	
	Existing Group	A-works	
	Description	Required engineers	
	Display choices using	Checkboxes (allow multiple selections)	
	Allowed Values	Construction engineer	
		Electro-technical engineer	
		Safety engineer	
		High pressure specialist	
	Default value	<blank>	

Table 4.2: Values for Site columns of content type Installation manual

Retention policy

1. 3 years after creation: remove old work versions

2. Immediately after approval: retention (15 years)

3. After expiry of the retention term: destruction

Content type hub

SharePoint has a layered construction, and content types may be defined at various levels and locations:

- In site collections
- In (sub)sites
- In the content type hub

The content type hub was introduced in SharePoint 2010 as a central location for the creation of content types, as a counterpart to the decentralized definition in site collections and (sub)sites.

The best location for the creation of content types is the content type hub. The retention schedule is a central document in the organization, for which top management carries the responsibility (although this responsibility will be delegated in practice). It is therefore sensible to create its translation in SharePoint at a single location as well. Adjustments in the retention schedule will then lead to adjustments at a single location in SharePoint rather than adjustments in various locations, by various people. This facilitates management. In addition, it is easier to check in SharePoint whether the retention schedule has been fully and correctly implemented. Troubleshooting and technical maintenance are much easier when records are defined at a central location. The prefix ACTH in the workable demo makes clear that it concerns content types that are defined in the A-Works content type hub. This way, site collection administrators and site owners know that they cannot adjust these content types.

The content type hub works according to a so-called 'publish-subscribe' model. This means that the sites may 'subscribe' to the content types that are published in the content type hub. Not only does this mean that the content types need to be created centrally, but also that the various sites, including the record center, will have to subscribe.

Based on the foregoing, we choose to apply the content type hub in order to create the definition of the content types. This introduces a fourth element in our design, see Figure 4.2.

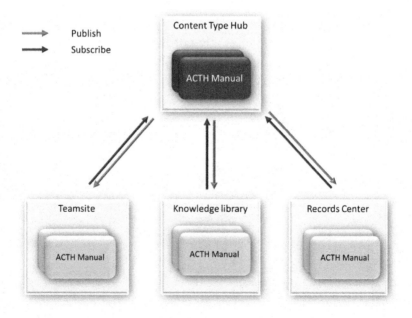

Figure 4.2: Elements of the solution after adding the content type hub

Records center

The records management system of A-works, which is the focus of this chapter, is implemented in SharePoint with a records center. This is a specialized site collection. As an alternative to the record center, it would also have been possible to base a solution on in-place records management (to be discussed later). In this case, a records center is the most logical solution, in view of our criteria: after the records have been included in the records center, they can no longer be accidentally used by engineers, and they are easy to access for staff in the legal affairs department. If in-place records management were used, the documents would still be among the active documents.

Based on their content type, records are grouped in document libraries in the record center. The routing of the records is defined by the creation of rules in the drop-off library. This is a specialized document library to which the records are sent with the help of the 'send to' mechanism. Figure 4.3 provides a graphic representation for our case. It is not always necessary to create an individual document library for each content type. When convenient from a business perspective, various content types may be combined in a single folder.

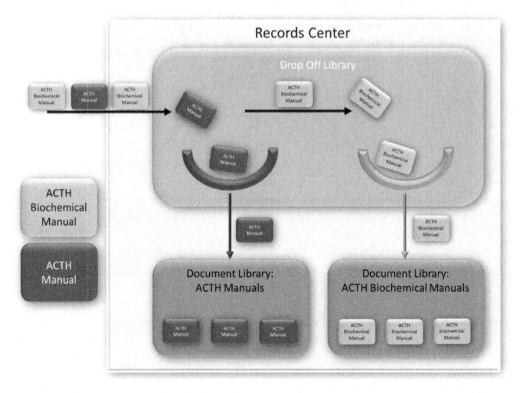

Figure 4.3: Rules for the routing of records based on the content types

Overview of the design

We have now seen four key elements in our design:

- Content type hub
- Team site
- Knowledge library
- Records center

The communication between the various elements is shown in Figure 4.4. 'Publish-subscribe' means passing on the definitions of the content types (the figure only shows an ACTH Manual). 'Publish-subscribe' takes place between the content type hub and the A-Works site collection. 'Send to' is sending a document to another site. Both types of relationships require configuration in SharePoint.

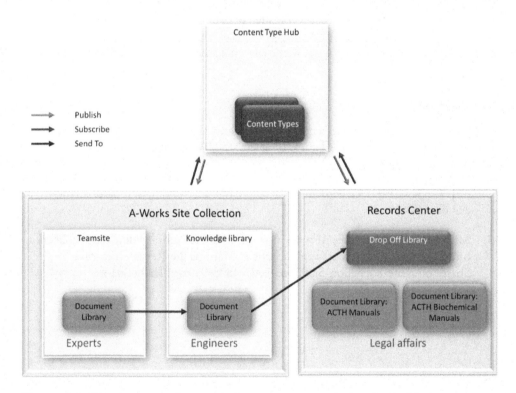

Figure 4.4: The elements of the records management solution for A-Works

In Figure 4.4, a fifth design element is added: the A-Works site collection. This is the container in which the team site and the knowledge library are both included. We will later see that this is convenient, because the similarities between these two play a role in the 'publish-subscribe' of the content type and the 'send to' location. In a more complex situation, there may be reasons to keep the two apart, when the differences between the team site and the knowledge library are foremost. Figure 4.4 shows that the records center in SharePoint is also a site collection.

There are similarities in terms of configuration between the A-Works site collection and the site collection for the records center, as far as the configuration of the 'publish-subscribe' relationship and the 'send to' locations is involved.

> SharePoint design rule: when the similarities between two sites are foremost, place them in the same site collection. When there are major differences which translate into different settings at the site collection level, then opt for several site collections.

References

1. SharePoint, Enterprise Architecture and anything between. Alfred de Weerd. http://www.alfreddeweerd.com/Blog/Post/2/Architectural-principles

2. SharePoint, Enterprise Architecture and anything between. Alfred de Weerd. http://www.alfreddeweerd.com/Blog/Post/4/SharePoint-standard-versus-custom--8---2

3. Microsoft. Manage the Recycle Bin of a SharePoint Online site collection. https://support.office.com/en-au/article/Manage-the-Recycle-Bin-of-a-SharePoint-site-collection-5fa924ee-16d7-487b-9a0a-021b9062d14b

Chapter 5

Workable demo: configuration

In the previous paragraphs, we discussed the requirements for the case, and saw their consequences for the design. In this chapter, we will implement the design by means of configuration of SharePoint. The focus will be on discussing the various options within SharePoint and their relation to the records management practice from the previous chapters. In contrast to many other texts, the solution is particularly in line with the records continuum. SharePoint is the most suitable for this, if only because it is a combined document management and records management system.

During the configuration of a records management solution, it is easy to lose sight of the bigger picture. This is because various elements of SharePoint are involved, which cannot be configured separately. After a number of steps in one part, something needs to be done in another part, forcing you to jump back again. In the workable demo we are going to create in this chapter, I have ensured that the steps are grouped by key area for the sake of clarity.

Even if you are not interested in the details at this point, it is advisable to read the considerations regarding the configuration sections provided in this chapter. This allows you to see how requirements form a basis for the records management solution, what considerations determine the design, and what factors play a role in the configuration of SharePoint.

The configuration includes the steps shown in Figure 5.1.

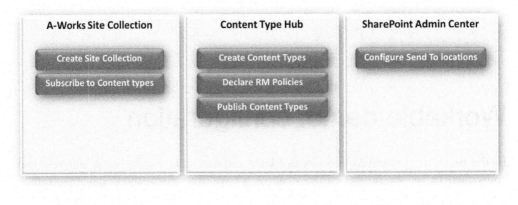

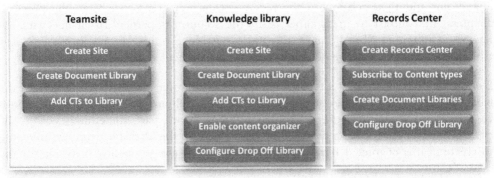

Figure 5.1: The steps in the configuration of the workable demo: Records management for A-Works

When configuring the workable demo, consider the following:

- Rights will be required, relating to the areas described in Figure 5.1, such as: Team site, Knowledge library and Records Center. In practical terms, this means: Creating a site collection and having the related site collection owner rights, creating a records center and having the necessary site collection rights there, as well as having SharePoint administrator rights allowing access to the SharePoint admin center. Perhaps there is a test environment where you can obtain these rights, or you may request the SharePoint administrator to perform certain steps. An alternative is to apply for a SharePoint Online environment. A plan1 or plan2 environment may be applied for at a cost of 5 to 8 dollars a month, in which the workable demo may be configured without the help of the IT department. See the Microsoft site for more information (*1*).
- There are a few steps after which there will be a waiting period, for example after creating a records center.
- The steps in this chapter are based on SharePoint Online as part of Office 365. For SharePoint 2010 and 2013 On Premise, the steps are largely the same, although deviations are possible.
- This workable demo has been set up in such a way that the configuration is

linear, despite the fact that it includes quite a number of steps. By making other design choices, for example, in the area of 'send to records', the steps would have been mixed up. This is a consequence of the fact that, in this case, the Send to locations have to be set up, before the retention rule can be created.

Configurations in the Content Type Hub

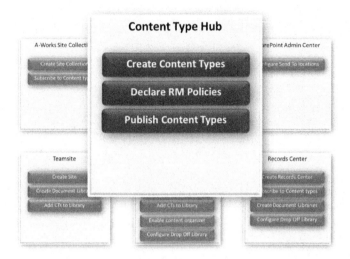

With an on premise SharePoint Server, the creation and configuration of a content type hub starts with central administration. As this is a book for business staff, end users and consultants, we will not discuss this task here. The steps are described in many places online, see for example (2). In SharePoint Online it is much easier: The site is already configured by default. The only problem is to find it. This is not a joke: there is no direct link to the content type hub in an administrator menu. Instead, you can determine the (standard) address as follows: https://<tenant>.sharepoint.com/sites/contenttypehub. The tenant is the instance of Office 365 for a specific (sub)organization. Every tenant has its own basic address, for example: www.alfreddeweerd.com.

Creating content types

The properties of the two content types in this workable demo – manual and biochemical manual – are described in the design. Perform the following steps to create and configure them in the content type hub:

1. Go to the content type hub by typing https://<tenant>.sharepoint.com/sites/contenttypehub in the address bar. The tenant is the name of the SharePoint Online environment as applied for at Microsoft

2. Select the Options button ⚙ in the top right corner, and then **Site Settings**

3. Under **Web Designer Galleries**, select **Site Content Types**

4. Select **Create**, above the list of Site Content Types

5. Fill in the first screen as indicated in Figure 5.2 and select **OK**.

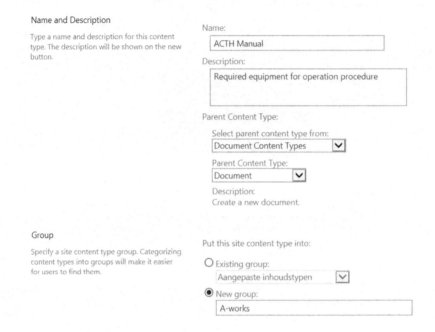

Figure 5.2: Creating the ACTH Manual content type

6. Select **Add from new site column** in the screen that opens (the configuration screen for the content type). This way, you create a new site column that will be re-used in the next content type.

7. Enter the values as described in the content type section of the design. For the sake of convenience, they are also displayed in Figures 5.3 and 5.4. Select **OK**

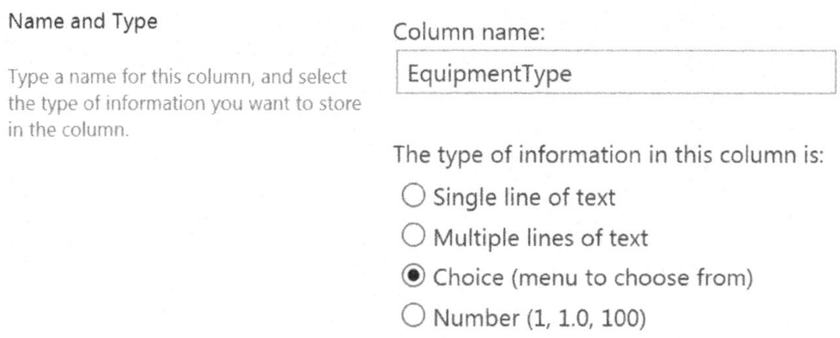

Name and Type

Type a name for this column, and select the type of information you want to store in the column.

Column name:

EquipmentType

The type of information in this column is:

○ Single line of text

○ Multiple lines of text

◉ Choice (menu to choose from)

○ Number (1, 1.0, 100)

Figure 5.3: Creating EquipmentType column, first part

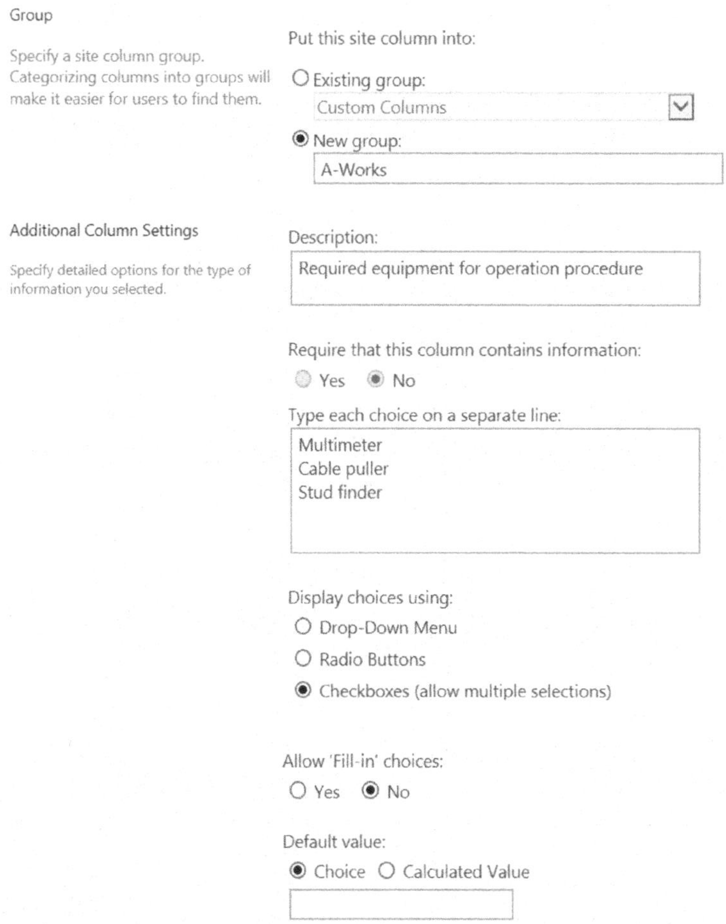

Group

Specify a site column group. Categorizing columns into groups will make it easier for users to find them.

Put this site column into:

○ Existing group:
Custom Columns

◉ New group:
A-Works

Additional Column Settings

Specify detailed options for the type of information you selected.

Description:

Required equipment for operation procedure

Require that this column contains information:
○ Yes ◉ No

Type each choice on a separate line:

Multimeter
Cable puller
Stud finder

Display choices using:
○ Drop-Down Menu
○ Radio Buttons
◉ Checkboxes (allow multiple selections)

Allow 'Fill-in' choices:
○ Yes ◉ No

Default value:
◉ Choice ○ Calculated Value

Figure 5.4: Creating EquipmentType column, second part

8. Repeat steps 6 and 7 for the columns 'Installation' and 'Engineer'.

We base the ACTH biochemical manual content type on the ACTH manual. In this case, we do this to limit the typing work somewhat. In a realistic scenario, you do this in order to provide the content types with a common basis. In this case, you would have a content type *A-Works document* with all metadata that applies to all of A-Works, and perhaps a content type *Manual,* based on an A-Works document, with metadata that applies to all manuals. See also *Chapter 8: Metadata and taxonomy.*

Follow the next steps for the configuration of the ACTH biochemical manual:

1. Select **Create**, above the list of Site content types

2. Fill in the first screen as indicated in Figure 5.5 and select **OK**.

Name and Description

Type a name and description for this content type. The description will be shown on the new button.

Name:

ACTH Biochemical Manual

Description:

Required equipment for operation procedure on Biochemical installation

Parent Content Type:

Select parent content type from:
A-works

Parent Content Type:
ACTH Manual

Description:
Required equipment for operation procedure

Group

Specify a site content type group. Categorizing content types into groups will make it easier for users to find them.

Put this site content type into:

⦿ Existing group:
A-works

○ New group:
A-works

Figure 5.5: Creating the ACTH Biochemical Manual

Configuring records management policies

In this step, we are going to implement the retention policy for the document types ACTH manual and ACTH biochemical manual. This is done in SharePoint by defining one or more retention stages, which consist of an event and an action.

Unfortunately, only a few events are available by default:

- Created: The date on which the document was created.
- Modified: The date of the (last) change to the document.
- Declared record: The date on which the document was declared a record. In SharePoint, it is possible to declare a document record manually, but it can also be done automatically. When declared a record, it can no longer be removed, relocated or modified in the usual way. See also in this chapter: *In-place records management*.

Every retention stage is based on one of these three dates. It is possible to define other events by means of customization. If the document has undergone several changes, the last modification date is used. If another change occurs after the calculation of the retention period, there will be no recalculation.

The available actions are included in Table 5.1. When applying the actions, the item may already be a record, but it may also still be a document. Not only can retention stages be applied to records, but also to documents. It is not required that the document eventually ends up in the record stage. This may prove very useful, for example, in the event of removal of 'information with temporary value' a number of years after the last amendment.

Action	Description
Move to Recycle Bin	Application: The item needs to be removed, but there is an uncertainty that requires it to be possible to restore the document. An example of this is the automatic removal of outdated information. As a rule, owners of the information will be informed that their outdated information is about to be removed, in which case they will be enabled to secure their important documents. It may happen, of course, that an important document is overlooked. Should it appear that somebody still needs the information it must still be possible to cancel the removal. This is possible because the document/record is moved to the recycle bin. It is basically removed, but still available for emergencies. After a certain period, the recycle bin is emptied and removal is final.
Permanent Delete	Application: The item needs to be removed permanently. An example of this is the removal of personal data in accordance with legal provisions. These provisions generally require the complete irreversible deletion of the personal data. Another application is the removal of the document where it is certain that it no longer has any value for the organization, the owner or others at the time of removal.

Transfer to another location	Application: Sending a document to the records center, where it becomes a record. In addition, documents can also be relocated to other libraries as part of their life cycle. We also do this in this demo, but we use a manual action here.
Start a workflow	Application: If a number of sequential actions need to be performed before the document ends up in the next life stage. An example of this is the combination of an approval workflow that ends with sending the document to the records center. Workflows are often also used when one or more actions need to be performed that cannot be realized with standard SharePoint functionality
Skip to next stage	Application: Add extra time before a next retention stage commences.
Declare record	Application: Turns a document into an in-place record (see this chapter: In-place records management. From that time on, it can no longer be removed or relocated. Only administrators can cancel this with the help of 'undeclare record'. This action is only available when the option is activated in the right locations (described later on).
Delete previous drafts	Application: When not all old versions are relevant anymore, but when the most important versions still have to be retained. 'Delete previous drafts' removes all prior minor versions (interim version, indicated after the dot), prior to the last major version (indicated before the dot). So if a document has the following versions: • 1.2 • 1.1 • 1.0 • 0.1 Then only version 0.1 is removed with 'delete previous draft' and so the following versions remain: • 1.2 • 1.1 • 1.0 Draft versions may be removed to reduce storage costs. Contrary to popular belief, storage costs may be relevant. When working on an Office document that is already in the document library, a new version is created whenever

	'store' is pressed. Sometimes this involves tens of versions. Another underlying aim may be to remove potentially incriminating information, thus minimizing risks in the event of eDiscovery.
Delete all previous versions	Application: Removal of all previous versions. This could be used in the event that the record is not so much about capturing the actions, but when only the end result matters. This may be the case with contracts, for example. Just as with 'delete previous drafts', the underlying aim may be the freeing up of space. 'Delete all previous versions' removes all previous minor and major versions, starting from the last major version. So if a document has the following versions: • 2.1 • 2.0 • 1.1 • 1.0 • 0.1 Then versions 0.1, 1.0 and 1.1 are removed, so that the following versions remain: • 2.1 • 2.0

Table 5.1: Actions for retention of records

Recurrence

It may also be indicated in the dialogue window for the retention stage whether the action needs to be repeated. This option is only available for 'Delete previous drafts' and 'Delete all previous versions'. This makes sense for these actions: In many cases, the important thing is that the versions are permanently removed. By means of recurrence, subsequently created versions are also removed by a repeated removal action.

Transition from document to record

Less important documents will never become a record. SharePoint has two options available for documents that are sufficiently important:

- Declare the record manually or by means of a retention stage on the document. The date of this event may trigger subsequent actions, such as copying to the records center or destroying drafts.

- Send the document to a document library, where every new item is automatically declared a record, for example in a records center.

The term 'record' refers to the SharePoint definition here: A document that can no longer be modified, removed or relocated, and which acquires the status of 'record' by means of an explicit action. Of course, this relates to the significance of the document: does it include important information that may serve as evidence? A document in SharePoint terms could still be a record according to the definition of ISO 15489. In this case, we need to adopt a different approach to ensure that it cannot be removed, modified or relocated. It is easy to arrange for this in SharePoint by not allocating these rights to anyone – except to the administrators perhaps.

With this knowledge in mind, we are now going to configure the retention policy of the ACTH manual. The translation of this retention policy, as specified in the design according to the rules in SharePoint, is perhaps not immediately self-evident. Let us look at the rules once more:

1. *3 years after creation: Remove old work versions*

2. *Immediately after approval: Retain (10 years)*

3. *After expiry of retention term: Destroy*

Rule 1 is translated in our workable demo with the rule *Delete all previous drafts* after a day. We select this term in the workable demo rather than three years because we want to see the impact of our configuration.

Rule 2 and 3 combined find their translation in the rule *Move to recycle bin*, two days after the declaration as a record. So the fact that the record needs to be retained does not have to be indicated explicitly in a rule. In this case, the trigger takes place two days after the declaration as a record. We have seen already that declaring a record may be done manually, but also by sending the document to the record center, where it is automatically declared a record. We selected the second option in the workable demo.

Follow the steps below to configure the retention policy:

1. Go to https://<tenant>.sharepoint.com/sites/contenttypehub

2. Select the Options button ⚙ ,in the top-right corner and then **Site Settings**

3. Under **Web Designer Galleries**, select **Site content types**

4. Select ACTH Manual

5. Under **Settings**, select **Information management policy settings**

6. In the Edit Policy page that now opens, fill in the following values:

    a. Administrative description: Policy for the ACTH Manual

b. Policy statement: Policy according to Retention policy 1.0

7. Select Enable retention

8. Click on Add retention policy

9. Fill in the values as indicated in Figure 5.6:

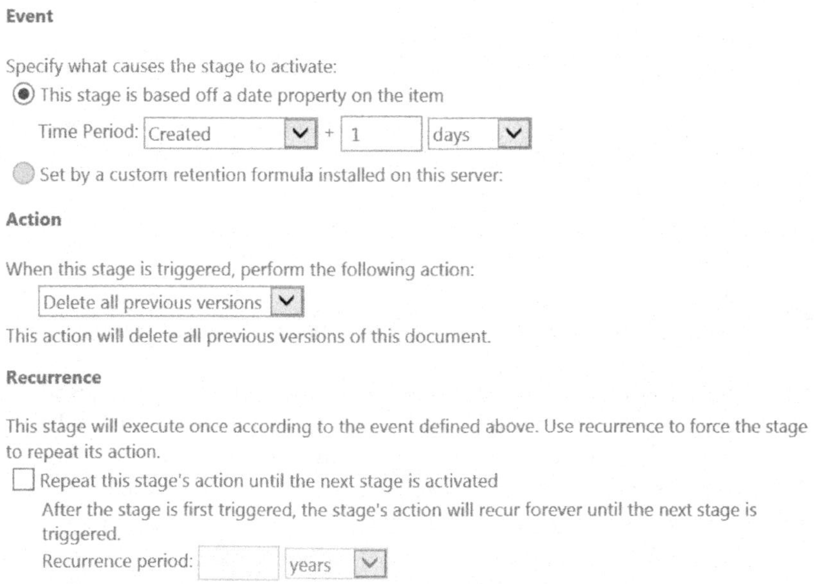

Event

Specify what causes the stage to activate:

◉ This stage is based off a date property on the item

Time Period: | Created ▾ | + | 1 | days ▾ |

◯ Set by a custom retention formula installed on this server:

Action

When this stage is triggered, perform the following action:

| Delete all previous versions ▾ |

This action will delete all previous versions of this document.

Recurrence

This stage will execute once according to the event defined above. Use recurrence to force the stage to repeat its action.

☐ Repeat this stage's action until the next stage is activated

After the stage is first triggered, the stage's action will recur forever until the next stage is triggered.

Recurrence period: | | years ▾ |

Figure 5.6: Creating a retention policy for the ACTH Manual

10. Repeat steps 8 and 9 and fill in the values shown in Figure 5.7

11. Click on **OK**

12. Repeat steps 4 up to 12 for the ACTH Biochemical Manual, see Figures 5.6 and 5.7

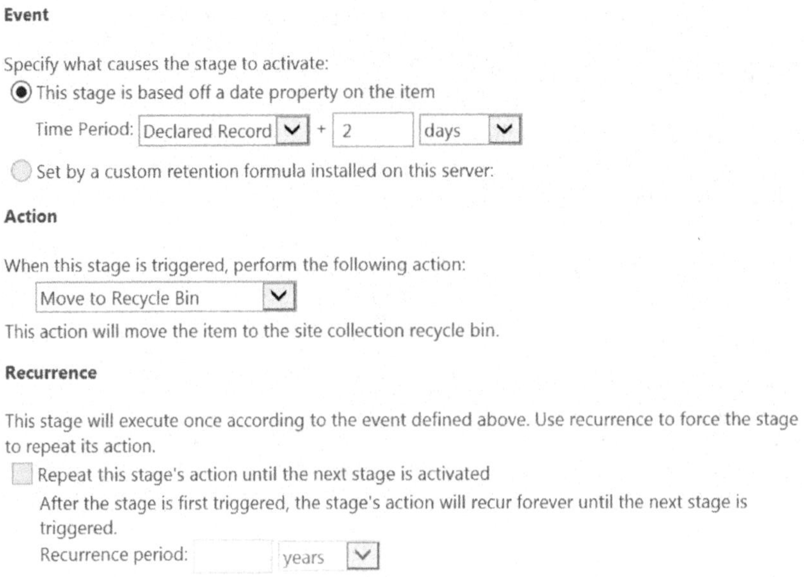

Event

Specify what causes the stage to activate:

◉ This stage is based off a date property on the item

Time Period: | Declared Record ⌄ | + | 2 | | days ⌄ |

◯ Set by a custom retention formula installed on this server:

Action

When this stage is triggered, perform the following action:

| Move to Recycle Bin ⌄ |

This action will move the item to the site collection recycle bin.

Recurrence

This stage will execute once according to the event defined above. Use recurrence to force the stage to repeat its action.

☐ Repeat this stage's action until the next stage is activated

After the stage is first triggered, the stage's action will recur forever until the next stage is triggered.

Recurrence period: | | years ⌄ |

Figure 5.7: Creating a retention policy for the ACTH Biochemical Manual

When testing, bear in mind that SharePoint Online executes the policies about once a week. The implementation is set internally by two timer jobs that expire. In SharePoint on Premise, they may be set so that they expire daily, which simplifies testing. Search on the Internet for 'Expiration policy' and 'Information management policy' to see how the setting of these timer jobs needs to be adjusted in Central Administration.

Because the retention policy is configured for the ACTH manual, this is also done automatically for the ACTH biochemical manual. The retention terms are now the same. This could also have been solved in a different way, namely by reusing the metadata of a higher-level content type in a different way. We call this inheritance, as can be seen in Figure 5.8. See also *Chapter 8: Metadata and taxonomy*. In order to reduce the amount of work, we did not do this in this workable demo.

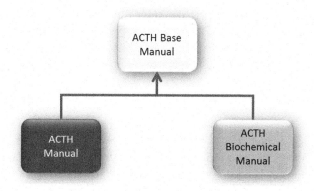

Figure 5.8: Inheritance of content types

Logic and specifics of retention rules

A particular logic applies to the execution of the retention rules, which is described below. A number of these logic rules were discussed before and are now added again, so that all the rules of logic are combined.

Order of execution

The rules are executed from top to bottom. This seems logical, but it is possible to configure the rules in such a way that a certain rule has an earlier execution date than the one above it. In these cases, the top one is still implemented first. It will be quite confusing to configure the rules in this way.

Frequency of execution

In SharePoint Online, the retention rules are executed on a weekly basis. In SharePoint on premise, this may be configured in a daily execution, for example. This is certainly useful for testing and demonstrations.

Simultaneity of execution

If, according to the configuration, two rules would have to be implemented on the same date (or in the same week for SharePoint Online), only the upper rule will be executed. The lower rule will have to wait until the next time the timer goes off. I have the impression that an exception is made here sometimes, and that both rules are executed, but I am not entirely sure of this.

Rules for records and non-records

If the content types are defined in a site collection where the in-place records management feature is activated as well, separate rules may be created for records and non-records. When a document of such a content type is not yet declared a record, the rules from the group of non-records are executed. When the document is subsequently declared a record, the rules from the group of records apply. It is also possible to apply the same rules to records and non-records. When the action *Declare record is used*, a switch is made to the rules for records. This is also the case when other rules are listed after the rule in which the record is declared. These actions are never executed in this case. If it is not necessary to define separate rules, it is best not to activate this option. This reduces the risk of unintentionally skipping rules. Yet other unintended effects may occur, see the next item.

Copy and move

The section *Defining a Send to location for the A-Works records center* in this chapter describes that there are three ways to send a document to another document library via a drop off library (see also the drop off library for more details):

- Copy. Makes a copy of the item in the new location.
- Move. Moves the document to the new location. No version remains.
- Move and leave a link. Moves the document to the new location, but leaves a link.

For a document, all three options are available. If, however, the document is declared a record at the time of relocation, the rules of *Move* and *Move and leave a link* will not be executed, as records cannot be moved manually. This becomes evident when you select the Compliance details of the record in the menu. 'Action' will then specify: *Invalid retention stage*. In this case, the *SharePoint System account* placed a lock on the document, as a result of which you are unable to move it as a user. System account itself is able to (automatically) relocate, because the lock is then lifted.

If a record, via a drop off library, is sent to a document library where declaring records is not allowed (this may be set in the configuration of the document library), the record symbol does appear in the document library, but the compliance details of the item will indicate that it is not a record. The status of the document is therefore unclear. So if you want to send a record to another document library, make sure the target library is configured to allow the declaration of records.

In the site collection settings menu you will find the record declaration settings. You will see there that the default setting for record restrictions at site collection level is: *Block edit and delete*. This setting must not be changed in any event, otherwise in-place records management is undermined (in place records may then be modified, which is highly irregular). The result is that a record that is sent to another library with *Move and leave a link* can no longer be adjusted in the source library, even though a lock is no longer displayed.

If an item is relocated to another library with *Move and leave a link*, the last version (whether this is a major or minor version) is the 1.0 version in the target library. In the source library, all versions prior to the last one are removed. SharePoint automatically adds two new minor versions. This is because the actual document is replaced with a link. Why there should be *two* new versions, only the technicians of Microsoft know. The standard functionality 'send to' therefore does not allow a document and all its versions to be relocated to the records center in a single action. This is a gap in the functionality that is hopefully soon filled by Microsoft.

When it is important to retain the old versions as part of the records, the design does need to properly take this into account. A possibility is to send every version separately to the records center, which will keep track of the various versions on site. The option *Copy* needs to be used for this, as with *Move and leave a link*, adjustments can no longer be made. The document itself is sent to the records center and can no longer be adjusted there. It is still possible to amend the metadata of the remaining link that is displayed as a document. This metadata will actually have to be regarded as the metadata of the link, and not that of the document itself. Yet it is better not to do this is in order to avoid confusion.

When it has not been taken care of in the records center that documents are automatically declared a record (see also in this chapter: *Set automatic declaration of records*), the following behavior for versions will occur after selecting *Move and leave a link*: At the time of relocation, all versions are removed and the last version becomes version 1.0 in the records center. When selecting the document in the source library, the document is opened in the library within the records center. Modifications may now be made. These changes appear as new versions in the library in the records center, but are not visible in the source library. This makes sense, for only a link is listed here, and this link will not change. As indicated above, the metadata of the document (which is in fact only a link) can indeed be adjusted in the source library. Normally this option does not apply, because it is configured in the records center that the document is automatically declared a record. I have described it here all the same, for perhaps there is an application for it, which I have not yet discovered myself.

Removing drafts and versions

As indicated above, not all previous minor and major versions are removed, but only the ones that are older than the last published major version. See in this chapter: *Defining Records management policies*. If there is a new rule that removes the previous minor or major drafts again, and a new major version is added, the new situation will become the starting point.

Recurrent execution of rules

The option of recurrently executing a rule only seems useful for the removal of previous drafts or versions. It is of no use sending a document to the recycle bin when it is already there, or declaring it a record when this was done before. But in some situations it is useful, when previous versions are removed, to repeat this before the next step is implemented and new versions may have been created in the meantime.

Publishing content types

Publishing content types is simple:

1. In the content type hub, Select the Options button ⚙, in the top-right corner and then **Site**

Settings

2. Under **Web Designer Galleries**, select **Site content types**

3. Select ACTH Manual

4. Select **Manage publishing for this content type** and click on **OK**

Modifications and republication

After making modifications in a content type in the content type hub, the content type has to be published again explicitly, otherwise the modifications will not become visible in the sites that subscribed themselves. The reason is that a great deal may depend on the definition of the content types in the content type hub, perhaps more than the person that configured the changes initially thought. Explicit publication as an additional step creates an obstacle that ensures any changes implemented too readily do not immediately have far-reaching consequences. It is advisable to subject republication to the same minimal formal steps used for the initial publication. Republication is available in the configuration of the relevant content type, under **Manage Publishing for this content type**.

Creating a records center

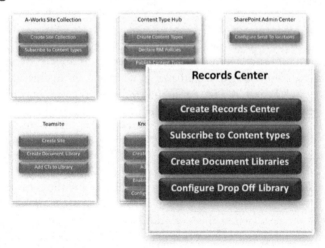

A records center is created with the help of a site template. The records center site template may be compared to other SharePoint-sites: It serves as the general storage location for documents and facilitates co-operation between site users. However, the records center site template is a pre-configured site, with functionalities that are unique to the records center. It is specifically designed to implement a records management system.

Follow these steps to create a records center:

1. Select the **program symbol** ▦ in the top-left corner

2. Select the **Admin** icon. If you do not see this icon, you do not have sufficient rights. Please contact the SharePoint administrator in this case. As indicated in the introduction, another option is to subscribe to Office 365 yourself. This is possible for a few euros a month.

3. Select **SharePoint** in the menu on the left side, under the heading **Admin**. A screen will open in which all existing site collections are displayed

4. Select **New** and then **Private site collection** on the Ribbon,

5. Enter the following details:

6. **Title**: A-Works Records center

7. **Web site address**: Do not change the checkboxes and fill in: *aworksrecordscenter* in the free text field

8. Under **Select a template**, select the tab **Enterprise** and then **Records center**

9. Add your own username under **Administrator**

10. Enter '500' under **Storage quota**. We do not need a great deal of space in the workable demo.

11. Do not change the other fields

There are many aspects of creating a site collection that are not covered by this book. More information can be found on the Internet:

- SharePoint Server 2013: see TechNet: Create a site collection in SharePoint 2013 (3)
- SharePoint Online: see Office Online: Create or delete a site collection (4)

Subscribe to content types

1. In the A-works Records center, click on the settings icon ⚙ in the upper right and then select **Site Settings** from the **drop down menu**

2. Select **Content type publishing** below Site collection administration

3. Tick the box before **Refresh all published content types** on next update and

Records Center

Create Records Center

Subscribe to Content types

Create Document Libraries

Configure Drop Off Library

press **OK**

Create document libraries

To create and configure a library to hold the manuals, follow these steps:

1. Go to the A-works Records Center

2. Click **Site Contents** on the left menu or click on the **settings icon** in the upper right (the wheel) and then select **Site Contents** from the **drop down menu**

3. Select **add an app**

4. Select **Document library**, name it *Manuals* in the window that pops up and select **Create**. The document library now appears next to the other lists and libraries. You may return to it later by again selecting **Site Content** and then clicking the Manuals document library.

5. In the Manuals document library, select **Library Settings** from the ribbon

6. Select Advanced Settings and then, below **Allow management of content types?**, select **Yes** and press **OK**

7. Below **Content types**, select **Add from existing site content types**

8. Add ACTH Manual and press OK

Set automatic declaration of records

To make the Manuals a record automatically in the document library (note that this is a trigger for the retention policy, defined by us in the design section), follow these steps:

1. Go to the A-works Records Center

2. Click **Site Contents** on the left menu or click on the **settings icon** in the upper right (the wheel) and then select **Site Contents** from the **drop down menu**

3. Select the **Manuals** document library

4. On the ribbon, select the **Library** tab and then **Library settings**

5. Select **Record declaration settings**, a page opens for the configuration of records declaration

6. Next to Automatic declaration, check the box with the text **Automatically declare items as records when they are added to this list**

7. Press **OK**

Create a document library for ACTH Biochemical Manuals

Repeat the steps as described above for ACTH Manuals. Name the document library Biochemical Manuals, add the content type ACTH Biochemical Manual and set the automatic declaration of records.

Once this configuration is complete, the staff at the Legal Affairs department can use all the functionality from document libraries to group, sort and filter records on the basis of metadata. They can also search in the records center.

Configure the Drop Off library

We are now going to create rules so that ACTH Manuals and ACTH Biochemical Manuals are automatically forwarded to the right document library. If you forgot how this works, you may want to refer back to the previous chapter, where we designed the *Record Center*, and especially Figure 4.3.

1. Go to the A-works Records Center

2. Click on the **settings icon** in the upper right (the wheel) and then select **Site settings** from the **drop down menu**

3. Select **Content organizer rules**, below Site administration

4. In the screen that opens up, select **New Item**

5. Name the rule ACTH Manual, select the ACTH Manual as the content type and the Manuals document library as the destination

6. Repeat steps 4 and 5 for the ACTH Biochemical Manual, selecting the Biochemical Manuals document library as the destination

The rules in the drop off library can be extended with conditions. Without conditions, all items of a content type are forwarded to the specified document library. Conditions may be applied to make a distinction in the target location, for example on the basis of the engineering role. It is important, however, to exercise caution here. If records are sent to the wrong library, it may in the real world take years before this is discovered, and often only after extensive research. Sending records to a different library is particularly useful when there are fundamental differences between the libraries. This may involve differences in accessibility between the user groups, different methods for ordering information and so on. Another good reason to make a distinction is when the libraries threaten to become too large. Creating order is not a strong reason in itself. When the other features are the same, it is preferable to create order by grouping, sorting and filtering on the basis of metadata, whether or not in combination with available views. When the treatment of records of a content type strongly depends on the value of a certain property, this often indicates that it actually involves a different document type. It would therefore have to be implemented with a different content type. This would have to be reported as feedback to those who created the retention schedule.

It is even possible to expand the rules in the drop off library in such a way that a new folder is created in the target library based on the value of a property. This may be necessary to prevent the library from becoming too large. As described above, the application of this option for the sake of establishing order is not such a good idea. A metadata-based organization in the library itself is much more flexible.

Optional: Giving users access rights

If the authorization hierarchy plays an important role in your working example, this is the time to give access rights to the right SharePoint group, for this site the legal affairs staff. To make this working demo not overly large, I have skipped this, assuming all sites can be accessed by the same persons. In general, working with access rights in a demo proves not to be very practical. You typically end up retyping usernames and passwords constantly, switching screens and confusing your audience and yourself.

Creating the A-Works site collection

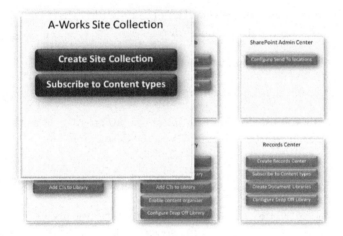

Follow these steps to create the A-Works site collection:

1. Select the **program symbol** ⊞ top-left corner

2. Select the **Admin** icon. If you do not see this icon, you do not have sufficient rights. Please contact the SharePoint administrator in this case. As already indicated in the introduction, another option is to take out a personal subscription to Office 365. This is possible for a few euros a month.

3. In the menu on the left side, select **SharePoint** under the heading **Admin**. A screen will open in which all existing site collections are displayed

4. Select **New** and then **Private site collection** on the Ribbon

5. Enter the following details:

    i.   **Title**: A-Works

    ii.   **Website address**: do not change anything in the checkboxes and fill in 'aworks' in the free text field

6. Under **select a template**, select the tab **Collaboration** if it is not already selected by default, and select **Team site**

7. Under **Administrator** insert your username

8. Enter '500' under **Storage quota**. We do not need a great deal of space in the workable demo.

9. Do not change anything in the remaining fields

Subscribe to content types

1. In the A-works site collection, click on the settings icon ⚙ in the upper right and then select **Site Settings** from the **drop down menu**

2. Select **Content type publishing** below Site collection administration

3. Tick the box before **Refresh all published content types** on next update and press **OK**

If the content types do not appear in the site after a while, you might check the **Content type publishing error log**, on the same page. One of the problems that might occur is a name conflict between the content type or one of its columns in the content type hub and the subscribing site.

> When working in the A-works site collection, double check whether you are working on the right level, either the A-works site collection or one of the two subsites: Knowledge library or Expert site. It is easy to 'get lost' and problems arising from configurations at the wrong level are often difficult to trace and tedious to correct.

Create the knowledge library site

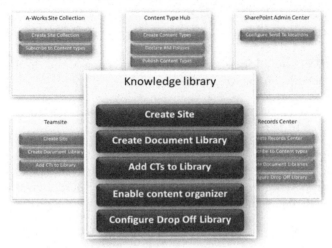

To create the knowledge library site, follow these steps:

1. In the A-works site collection, click **Site Contents** on the left menu or click on the **settings icon** in the upper right (the wheel) and then select **Site Contents** from the **drop down menu**

2. Select **New subsite** from the bottom of the page (scroll downward if required)

3. Fill in the fields:

    • Title: Knowledge site

    • Description: A-works knowledge site for operators

    • URLname: knowledge

    • Select a language: <set to your language>

    • Select a template: Team site (in the Collaboration tab)

4. Leave the other settings on their default values and select **Create**. After a few moments, your new knowledge library site will open. When you are at your top level site, the knowledge library will appear as a link on the top or on the left or both, depending on your navigating settings. If the knowledge library doesn't show up you can change the navigation settings of your top site, or you can return to your knowledge library by selecting **Site Contents** and then selecting your site under **sub sites**.

Create document library

To create a library follows these steps:

1. Go to your knowledge library site

2. Click **Site Contents** on the left menu or click on the **settings icon** in the upper right (the wheel) and then select **Site Contents** from the **drop down menu**

3. Select **Add an app**

4. Select **Document library**, give it a name in the window that pops up and select **Create**. The document library now appears next to the other lists and libraries. You may return to it later by again selecting **Site Content** and then clicking the new document library.

5. Select Advanced Settings and then, below **Allow management of content types?**, select **Yes** and press **OK**

6. Below Content types, select **Add from existing site content types**

7. Add ACTH Manual and press OK

8. Repeat steps 6 & 7 for the ACTH Biochemical Manual

In a more realistic demo, we would certainly want to enable the documents to be sorted and filtered on the basis of metadata. We did not do this in order to limit the length of the demo.

Enable the content organizer

From the previous chapter, where we designed the SharePoint solution, you might remember that Experts do their work on the Manuals in the Teamsite library and that, after they are done, the Manuals need to be sent to the Knowledge Library. Enabling the content organizer and configuring the Drop Off Library (next section) is what is needed to allow the Experts to send the finished manuals to the Knowledge Library. These two steps mean that an ACTH Manual and an ACTH Biochemical Manual are forwarded when put into the Drop Off Library, but a third step, defining Send to locations, is required to be able to send the manuals to the Drop Off Library in the first place. This is done later on in the step 'Defining a send to location for the knowledge library'. This may seem as a complicated way of configuring just the sending of documents from one library to the next but there are alternatives. These are discussed in the section 'An alternative to centrally defined 'send to''. You will see there we have taken the method above for a good reason.

To activate the Content Organizer feature for a site

1. In the A-Works Site Collection

2. Select **Options** ⚙ and then choose **Site Settings** from the drop down menu.

3. On the **Site Settings** page, in the **Site Actions** group, choose **Manage site features**.

4. Next to the Content Organizer feature name, click **Activate**. When the feature is activated, the word **Active** appears in the **Status** column

Configure the Drop Off library

At this point we are in the position to configure the drop off library. To do so:

1. Go to the A-works site collection

2. Click on the **settings icon** in the upper right (the wheel) and then select **Site settings** from the **drop down menu**

3. Select **Content organizer rules**, below Site administration

4. In the screen that opens up, select **New Item**

5. Name the rule ACTH Manual, select the ACTH Manual as the content type and the Knowledge Library as the destination

6. Repeat steps 4 and 5 for the ACTH Biochemical Manual, selecting the Biochemical Knowledge Library as the destination

Create a team site

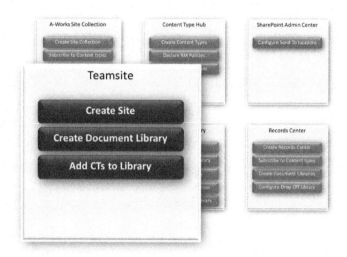

Creating the team site requires the same steps as *Create the knowledge library site*, described in the section above. Use the following data:

- Title: Experts site
- Description: Site for creation of Manuals by experts
- URLname: experts
- Select a language: <set to your language>
- Select a template: Team site (in the Collaboration tab)

Create a document library in the team site

Follow the instructions below *Create a document library* in the knowledge management site.

Optional: giving users access rights

If the authorization hierarchy plays an important role in your working example, this is the time to give access rights to the right SharePoint group for this site, the engineers. In order to make this working demo not overly large, I've skipped this, assuming all sites can be accessed by the same user. Keep in mind (and tell your audience) that you are assuming a different role for each site, however.

Configure Send to locations

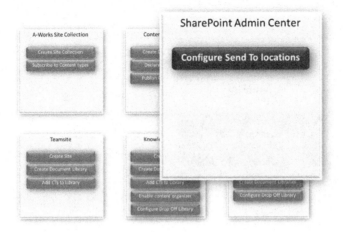

An essential operation in records management is sending documents to the records center. This starts the retention period. Sending a record to a different site collection can be enabled by configuration in the SharePoint Admin center. You do not have access to this as an ordinary user (fortunately), nor as a site owner or site collection owner. If you do not have access to the SharePoint admin center, please contact the SharePoint administrator.

Below I have described the required steps; not only do I describe what you can do, but also why you can do this:

1. In the Records Center, select the Options button ⚙ in the top-right corner and then **Site Settings**

2. Under Site Administration, select Content Organizer rules

3. Copy the Web Service URL, under Submission Points

4. Go to the SharePoint Admin Center and select Records management

5. Fill in the fields as indicated in the figure below (use the url of the content organizer of the Records Center) and click on **Add Connection**

Connection Settings

Each connection requires a display name and a URL to a content organizer. Optionally, this connection can be made available as a Send To option on the item's drop-down menu and on the Ribbon.

Display name:

| A-Works Records Center |

Send To URL:

| <Your URL> |

(Click here to test)
Example: "http://site url/_vti_bin/officialfile.asmx"

☑ Allow manual submission from the Send To menu

Send To action:

| Copy ▼ |

Explanation (to be shown on links and recorded in the audit log):

| Sends an item to the A-Works Records Center |

[Add Connection] [Remove Connection]

For 'send to' there are three options:

- Copy. Creates a copy of the item in the records center. There will then be two versions, one in the document library and one in the records center. The versions may start to differ from each other. This does not have to be a problem in the following situations:
    - We regard the version that is sent to the records center as a capture of the document at that point. The version that remains can be modified. If necessary, a new version may be sent to the records center as a separate document. This new version is then retained in the records center as a separate version.
    - The remaining version can no longer be modified (but using a *Move and leave a link* is more logical in this case).
- Move. Moves the document to the records center, as a result of which no version remains. This matches the scenario in which users also consider sending the record to the records center to be a logical conclusion of their activities.
- Move and leave a link. Moves the document to the records center. So there is only one version, which is situated in the records center. Users may still access it via the remaining link, at least if they have rights to the library in the records center.

Defining a send to location for the knowledge library

1. In the knowledge library site, select the Options button ⚙ in the top-right corner and then **Site Settings**

2. Under Site Administration, select Content Organizer rules

3. Copy the Web Service URL, under Submission Points

4. Go to the SharePoint Admin Center and select Records management

5. Fill in the fields as displayed in Figure 5.9 below (use the URL of the content organizer of the knowledge library) and click on **Add Connection**

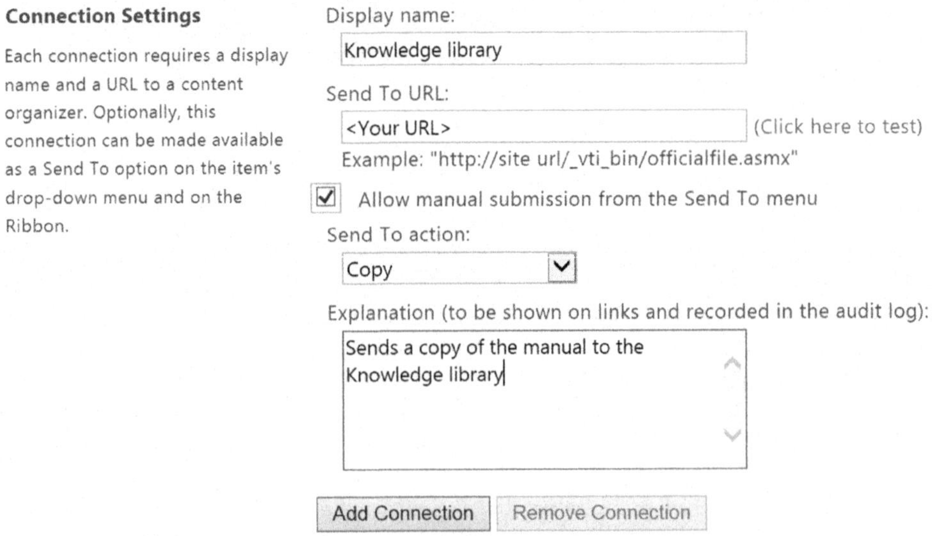

Connection Settings

Each connection requires a display name and a URL to a content organizer. Optionally, this connection can be made available as a Send To option on the item's drop-down menu and on the Ribbon.

Display name:

Knowledge library

Send To URL:

<Your URL>   (Click here to test)

Example: "http://site url/_vti_bin/officialfile.asmx"

☑ Allow manual submission from the Send To menu

Send To action:

Copy ▾

Explanation (to be shown on links and recorded in the audit log):

Sends a copy of the manual to the Knowledge library

Add Connection | Remove Connection

Figure 5.9: Defining the A-Works Records Center as a Send To location

An alternative to centrally defined 'send to'

Instead of defining the 'send to' in the central location in the SharePoint admin center, it may also be configured in the library itself. See Microsoft Office Online (5) for this. This 'send to' copies the files. It is not possible to use **Move** or **Move and leave a link**. But copying is carried out in such a way that the files are synchronized in the event of adjustments. In this sense, there are similarities with **Move and leave a link**. This is precisely the danger in our scenario, because a change in a Manual in the Expert library would automatically lead to a change in version in the Knowledge library, while the latter should be fixed at all times. So this would not be a good solution for our demo.

Conclusion

This concludes the configuration of the demo. The policy does not explicitly state that the records must be sent to the records center. This is a manual action. In a realistic situation, this action could be automated, but it is not required in a demo. It is even wise to implement the first version of a demo with standard functionality only, so that the necessity of customization may be considered. In addition, the benefits in terms of ease of use can be assessed better at a later stage, by comparing the standard version to a version without customization.

By default, only time-based events are available as triggers for the retention stages. I would have preferred that other events could be used, for example the completion of a version 1.0, but this is currently still a matter of customization.

The table below indicates how the various requirements are implemented in the solution.

No	Requirement	Implementation
1	Manuals that describe formal procedures based on laws and regulations need to be stored as records, retained for 10 years and subsequently destroyed	Records in the records center
2	Manuals of biochemical installations need to be retained for 15 years and subsequently destroyed	Records in the records center
3	Manuals are created through the collaboration of experts in SharePoint team sites (people who used to be engineers and subsequently also obtained knowledge of, among others, laws and regulations)	The experts team site that includes the document library
4	After formal approval, the manuals are added to the knowledge management system of A-works	No formal approval is implemented. A standard approval workflow can be quickly added, but there are so many configuration options that this is left out in this demo. Inclusion in the knowledge management system is arranged with 'send to'
5	There is only one active version of every manual in the knowledge management system	This should be done manually by the administrator of the knowledge library
6	Manuals in the knowledge management system can no longer be modified. Whenever	Is optionally added by giving engineers only reading rights to

	a change is required, a new manual is created, to which requirements 3 and 4 apply	the knowledge library
7	Only the staff of the legal affairs department should still have access to the versions of the records which are no longer used in the field	Is optionally added by only giving staff of the legal affairs department access to the libraries in the records center
8	Staff of the legal affairs department should be able to find the records on the basis of text search, and it should be possible to sort and filter them	Standard SharePoint search is available in the records center. Sorting and filtering is not displayed in this demo.

Table 5.2: Requirements for the knowledge library of A-Works and their realization

We see that most requirements are implemented. A number of requirements are not fully implemented or omitted for reasons of simplicity and because of the length.

It remains a broad solution in the current configuration which needs to be further configured and elaborated. An example of this is the application of versions. We do want this in the document library for experts, among others because errors are possible in the process of application of amendments, which may be rectified on the basis of older versions. We do not want this in the knowledge library in principle. After all, requirement E6 states that every change should lead to a new document. This may be enforced by not keeping track of versions. In this case, a warning will be given when a new document with the same name is added. There are many details like this one that have to be thought out and implemented in a real world solution.

In-place records management

Rather than using the records center, it is also possible to use in-place records management. In this case, records are not moved when they are declared a record. They remain present among the other records and documents in the library. It is also possible to integrate in-place records management in a broader records management solution, where the records are sent to the records center at a later stage.

An explanation of the various options follows below. We will first do the configuration. The settings for in-place records management are found in two locations:

- Site collection
- Library

Activating the feature

In order to be able to use In-Place Records Management, it will first be necessary to activate the feature In-Place Records Management. This is like turning the washing machine on before you can select a program. The required steps are as follows:

1. Go to the site collection

2. Select **Settings** ⚙, and then **Site Settings**

3. Under **Site Collection Administration**, click on **Site collection features**

4. Under **In Place Records Management,** select **Activate**

Configuring the site collection

1. Go to the site collection

2. Select **Settings** ⚙ , and then **Site Settings**

3. Under **Site Collection Administration**, click on **Record declaration settings**

4. On the Record Declaration Settings page, under **Record Restrictions**, check that **Block edit and delete** is selected

5. Under **Record Declaration Availability**, select **Not available in all locations by default**

6. Under **Declaration roles**, under **The declaration of records can be performed by,** check that **All list contributors and administrators** is selected

7. Also under **Declaration roles**, under **Undeclaring a record can be performed by,** check that **Only administrators** is selected

8. Select **OK**

At site collection level, the following parameters may be set:

- Limitations on records
- Option to declare records
- Declaration roles

For the limitations on records there are three options: No limitations, limit removal (only modifications are possible) and block editing and removal.

The latter option is the most obvious. It makes sense to only declare a document record when it is final. In these cases, editing and removal are no longer an issue. Moreover, this allows the record declaration to be canceled if necessary, should it prove to be unjustified at a later stage. Limit removal could be useful in some scenarios as well, especially when you are in a dynamic situation, where documents are to be regarded as records, while modifications are still possible.

With 'Option to declare records', it may be indicated whether or not management for in-place records should be available for all underlying libraries. If this is not selected, this may still be canceled at the library level, but this is not possible the other way around. So this is another master configuration switch. When turned off, no further configuration at lower levels is possible and this is just how it should be. When turned on, you would no longer be in control.

With declaration roles, we can indicate the roles that can manually declare and undeclare records. The default – all contributors and administrators can declare and only list administrators are able to cancel – reflects the most common practice. Case managers can decide on substantive grounds whether a document should become a record. Undeclaring a record is a relatively tough decision that could overturn the entire in-place records management system. This is why this option is only available to list administrators. The role of list administrator should be assigned to the right person, having the required business knowledge and authority.

Configuring the document library

1. Go to the document library

2. Select **Library settings** on the **Ribbon**

3. Click on Record declaration settings

4. Select **Automatically declare items as records when they are added to this list.**

These settings at library level are only available when the option 'make available in all locations by default' is selected at site collection level.

For the manual setting there are three options: Use the site collection default, always allow and never allow. The former will apply to the majority of the libraries. The second and the third option make exceptions to the policy that is defined at site collection level. This involves more administration. In addition, there is the risk that the library wrongly deviates from what was intended, at the site collection level.

Automatic declaration of in place records may be activated for all new items in the list. This may, for example, be useful in situations where incoming mail items immediately need to be declared records, for example in the event of official applications for permits and objections..

Records center or in-place records management

Having two possible solutions, it is sometimes difficult to choose between the records center and in-place records management. Although we have seen that it is not strictly necessary to exclude either of the two, it is nevertheless useful to have an overview of the benefits and drawbacks of each.

In-place records management

The central characteristic of in-place records management is that the records stay in the same location and that records and documents exist alongside one another.

Benefits have to do with ease of use and user experience:

- All versions in the lifecycle remain visible and accessible
- The document is not 'suddenly gone'
- Because other documents also remain, the context is preserved

Drawbacks have to do with security and a lack of structure and overview:

- When the records are distributed across various libraries, it is difficult to find all relevant records and enforce a shared policy or security system
- Sometimes you do not want records to remain visible and accessible. The A-Works demo is an example of this situation
- Because documents and records are intermingled, it may be unclear what the user is allowed to do with a document. The lock that is displayed when the editing and removal of records is forbidden only partially solves this. When searching and filtering, for example, both types end up mixed up, while users are often only interested in only one of the two. On the other hand, a great deal may be solved with various views
- The size of the document library increases more quickly

Records center

The benefits of the records center are a direct result of the structure and the related security options:

- All records can be easily found by the administrators of the records center
- A link may easily be created between the retention schedule and the records in the records center
- Access may be centrally arranged
- It is clear that all documents are records, and that they cannot be amended or removed
- The drop off library and the corresponding rules help to create structure, both at the level of libraries and within libraries
- A separate policy may be applied, specifically aimed at the records. This may include storage, backup regime and auditing

Drawbacks of the records center have to do with reduced accessibility and ease of use:

- When the transfer of records does not involve the provision of access to the records center, the document has become unfindable for users
- In the records center, the documents are taken out of their original context (although document sets may help), even when they are made available to the

users

- It may be difficult to make the documents available to the right groups of users without creating a complicated authorization hierarchy

Again: It is also possible to combine the use of the records center with in-place records management. In this case, the records center implements the more static stage of records, and in-place records management facilitates the more dynamic stage. A limitation here is that in-place records cannot be manually sent to the records center. Another limitation is that triggers for sending records to the records center are all time-based (creation date of the document, amendment date of the document, declaration date of the record). The combination of these two, for example, has resulted in the choice not to use in-place records in the workable demo. The trigger in this case is the availability of a new version of a manual in the knowledge library. This cannot be realized automatically without customization. The manual sending of in-place records to the records center is not possible either which, in view of the limited volume of the manuals, is a fine workable solution.

Archiving e-mail

Besides documents, e-mails may also contain important information, which may serve as evidence for best practices or compliance with laws and regulations. Unlike the archiving of documents, the archiving of e-mails is relatively new. This is not just because e-mails are newer than documents as a means of communication, but also because, for a long time, e-mails were not considered to be full-fledged information sources. All manner of approval layers are built in for documents and especially for important documents. They are printed on formal paper and various people are involved in their creation. E-mails, on the other hand, are often generated on an ad hoc basis by an individual person, after which they are usually sent without any further checks. E-mails can nevertheless be records. A few examples of important e-mails, both outgoing and incoming:

- Confirmation of a commercial agreement
- Confirmation of a price
- Making a formal proposal. The proposal itself will usually be included in an attachment, but the e-mail will contain essential metadata (see below)
- Complaints or other e-mails which serve as starting points for a case, or which are of importance for the progress of the case or a stage in it
- Communication about events or insights during a procedure which have an impact on the course of events

Because of their very nature, e-mails always contain the following, essential metadata:

- The address of the sender
- The address of the addressee
- The date

Just like documents, e-mails may serve as evidence in a lawsuit. In such cases, the reliability of e-mails will be thoroughly investigated. The question of whether digital signatures have been used and whether encryption has been applied will play a role here. So the reliability of e-mail may be debated.

Generally speaking, e-mails are not isolated messages, but form part of a communication process. E-mails would have to be included in an archive in such a way that they are related to the case in which they play a role. E-mails may therefore be important information sources, and it may be useful to treat them as such. In many cases, the information from e-mails emerges in documents created. This relieves the pressure on e-mails as record.

The standard location for mail archives is the personal desktop. This is highly undesirable from the perspective of security and availability of information. First of all, because e-mails are not safely stored on personal computers, where a crash of the hard drive will lead to loss of all data if there is no proper back-up. There is also a greater risk of theft and loss with personal computers and certainly laptops. Secondly, because information that is stored locally can no longer be simply retrieved on the basis of a central search query.

Exchange on Premise and Exchange Online

Archiving in Exchange was initially invented to limit the size of active mailboxes and to be able to store older, less often read e-mails separately. So, in this case, archiving does not immediately relate to the secure and controlled storage of records from the perspective of evidence provision. The aim is system stability and increased ease of use. The latter may, for instance, be achieved by the possibility of searching older e-mails in a self-selected manner and searching newer, more relevant e-mails separately. Users may create local files themselves (.pst files), in which they create their 'archive'.

With Exchange Online archiving, Microsoft creates an environment in which all e-mails can be archived. This corresponds with the principle from information management that information is processed and stored close to the source. This is less desirable from the perspective of building archive units from cases. In this regard, storing e-mails in the archive with the other documents – in our case SharePoint – is to be preferred, where they are always treated exactly the same as the other documents from the case. This applies both to the retention policy and to user operations such as searching and grouping.

Archiving in Exchange Online is included in various Office 365 license types and is available as an option for the remaining ones. It features Single Sign On (SSO) options in relation to Office 365. The storage capacity for Exchange Online archiving is unlimited (except for Exchange Online Plan 1 and Office 365 Midsize Business plans).

E-mail archive

The e-mail archive consists of an additional mailbox, which appears next to the other mailboxes of the user. The user can access the mailbox in the same way as the other mailboxes and search the archive.

The user can relocate e-mails from the ordinary mailboxes to the archive in various ways, among others by dragging and on the basis of retention rules. It is not possible to migrate e-mails with mailbox rules. Mail is moved to the archive, so the original is no longer visible in the original mailbox. This is a change compared to the previous version, Exchange Hosted Archive. The e-mail archive offers the option of restoring individually removed messages, or retrieving the entire mailbox. The e-mail archive is physically stored in various data centers that are located apart from one another. Additional business continuity management will be required to ensure that there safeguards against major disasters. Microsoft has included a clause in the service level agreement for Office 365, which makes them exempt from liability in the event of natural disasters, wars and acts of terrorism, see the Microsoft Office 365 SLA (6). However, it will be difficult for most companies to develop a security system that is better than that of Microsoft. The e-mail archive may be accessed with the Outlook Web App and Outlook 2010 or later versions. Outlook 2007 is more limited and only operates with part of the functionality.

Security

Exchange Online archiving standardly applies encryption to the traffic between Outlook users and the archive. Data in the archive may be stored in the format secure/multipurpose Internet mail extensions (S/MIME).

Messages may also be stored encrypted by using encryption on the side of the client, for example by means of pretty good privacy (PGP).

Exchange Online archiving supports the use of information rights management (IRM) by using active directory rights management services (AD RMS). This does have to be hosted on Azure. Office 365 Enterprise E3 and E4 users have access to AD RMS, and other users can purchase this as an additional option at two euro per user per month.

Auditing

Exchange Online archiving has two forms of auditing: One that is aimed at administrators and one that is intended for other users. The former is enabled by default, and the latter is disabled by default. The exchange admin center offers various standard audit reports.

Retention policy (messaging records management)

Administrators may create retention tags that contain a rule for archiving. Various tags may be combined to form a policy. A maximum of one policy may be applied to each mailbox otherwise it would become very complicated to determine what happens. By allocating a policy to a mailbox, the retention tags in that policy become applicable to specified folders. There are three types of retention tags (7):

- Retention policy tags: Administrators may assign these to standard folders, such as the inbox, sent and deleted items. Users can no longer edit or remove them.
- Personal tags: Users may apply them to self-made folders or to individual items in the standard folders. When users set a personal tag for an item or a folder, this takes priority over the generally assigned retention policy tag.
- Default policy tags: To prevent messages from slipping through the net, a default policy may be created, which applies to all folders or messages that were not assigned a tag explicitly or via inheritance.

Exchange Online features three actions that form the basis for the retention tags: 'archive', 'remove but keep available' and 'remove permanently'. Several tags may apply to every folder. A frequently occurring archiving scenario is that a message needs to be archived after a certain period and subsequently has to be removed.

Administrators themselves can directly apply the policy rules to the various folders, by means of retention tags, or by offering the rules to the user via personal tags, who then will have to apply the right option themselves. The latter is not ideal from an archiving perspective. Staff members make mistakes or standardly select the same value all the time when they do not recognize the use of archiving. On the other hand, the application of the policy rules by administrators is unrefined. The problem with e-mail is that the nature of the messages varies greatly, from messages about cake with your coffee to the final decision to accept a contract. A motivated user could therefore select the right archiving option for their e-mails themselves.

Journaling

Journaling is keeping a log of all e-mail communications as part of the archiving policy of an organization. Microsoft offers this option as part of the Exchange umbrella. The approach of retaining e-mails in such a way that they may be placed in the context of the total mail communication is in line with the records management principle that records need to be stored and be retrievable in the context. If the purpose is to store all records together, i.e. both documents and e-mails, then journaling will not be enough. But it could be a partial solution.

The actual archive is formed by a journal mailbox. At the time of writing, this could not yet be an Exchange online mailbox.

Archiving e-mail in SharePoint

The first question we need to answer in the case of archiving: Is the e-mail archived in Exchange or in SharePoint? As indicated before, the choice of Exchange means that the e-mail is disconnected from the other elements of a file, while in SharePoint this connection is preserved. In addition, SharePoint has the advantage that the functionality available for the other records, such as searching, grouping, filtering and sorting, can also be applied to the e-mail messages. Another advantage is that additional metadata may be added to the e-mails. So SharePoint supplies the more advanced records management solution, which is reinforced by the fact that e-mails are treated in the same way as the other documents in the implementation of the retention policy. Exchange does not necessarily need to be worse, but because of the way Exchange handles records management, it does differ at the implementation level. Because records management is spread over two systems, there also has to be records management expertise for these two systems.

Exchange has the great advantage that it is fully equipped for the archiving of e-mails. Unfortunately, this is not yet the case for SharePoint. The standard functionality does facilitate a few things, but in my experience the existing functionality is often not enough. External tools that ensure a smoother integration of SharePoint and Exchange, which have a high degree of user-friendliness are available. Of course, this also involves the well-known drawbacks of tools, such as purchase costs, problems occurring with new versions of SharePoint and the acquirement of knowledge of the tools, which has to be obtained within the company or sourced externally. In situations where there is no need for storing e-mail-based records alongside other records, Exchange is the ideal solution.

SharePoint Online offers the team site as a means of integration between Exchange and SharePoint. A site mailbox may be created in SharePoint with the help of an app named *Keep mail in context*. This makes it possible to send mail directly to the e-mail address belonging to the site mailbox. The e-mails are stored in Exchange. In SharePoint, it is possible to directly open the corresponding mailbox. The integration in Outlook goes further. Both the mailbox and the document library that is connected to the mailbox may be viewed. The functionality does not seem to be very useful. I have not been able to come up with practical scenarios. In a physical sense, e-mails and documents remain separated. From a functional perspective too, the functionality has little added value. A solution that has existed ever since SharePoint 2007 is the application of e-mail enabled lists. This functionality is not available for SharePoint Online. This solution also has limitations, as a result of which it is only suitable for very small-scale applications. There are a number of other methods for incorporating e-mail in SharePoint, which all have considerable drawbacks.

The conclusion: Full SharePoint functionality will be available once e-mail is included in SharePoint. For realistic scenarios, an additional tool will be required. Fortunately, there are a number of them, of which Colligo is probably the most well-known. You will find more information on their website (*8*).

References

1. Microsoft. Compare SharePoint options. https://products.office.com/en-us/sharepoint/compare-sharepoint-plans

2. Jean Paul on C-sharp corner. Create Content Type Hub in SharePoint 2013 http://www.c-sharpcorner.com/UploadFile/40e97e/create-content-type-hub-in-sharepoint-2013/

3. Microsoft TechNet: Create a site collection in SharePoint 2013. http://technet.microsoft.com/en-us/library/cc263094(v=office.15).aspx

4. Microsoft Office Online: Create or delete a site collection. https://support.office.com/en-in/article/Create-or-delete-a-site-collection-3a3d7ab9-5d21-41f1-b4bd-5200071dd539

5. Microsoft Office Online: Specify a Send To destination for a library https://support.office.com/en-ca/article/Specify-a-Send-To-destination-for-a-library-f5db67a2-7ddb-48a9-a652-deada0e91c3a

6. Microsoft. Service Level Agreement Office 365. http://www.microsoftvolumelicensing.com/DocumentSearch.aspx?Mode=3&DocumentTypeId=37

7. Microsoft. Retention tags and retention policies. http://technet.microsoft.com/library/dd297955.aspx

8. Colligo. http://www.colligo.com/sharepoint-solutions/business/records-management/

Chapter 6

Case management and records

management

In records management standards, such as ISO 15489, the starting point is that a group of documents should be declared records in such a way that their mutual relationship can still be traced, so that statistical and dynamic aspects of the case may be reproduced at a later stage. This may be done in various ways in SharePoint:

1. Include the documents in a document set and then send the entire document set to the records center. A document set is a neat digital folder and the comparison with a paper can be made quickly. A problem is that a document set itself cannot be declared as an in-place record. From a technical point of view, it has a content type derived from a folder, and it is not possible to apply in-place records management to this content type.

2. Assign a metadata field including a reference to another document. This could be a title, but in SharePoint it is more logical to use the document ID for this, as this is indeed unique. In this case, it is possible to use a document as the basis for a search for another document. This is a recommended practice in records management standards and in metadata standards.

3. Assign a metadata field including a reference to a unique case number, complaint number, handling code or something similar. This way, a view may be created in the target library in the records center which forms groups by case number. All documents belonging to a case are then grouped together.

4. Assume a substantive connection: a connection on the basis of content. This ensures that various documents may be found together in a search query. This solution makes some people nervous, because they wish to have the connection arranged formally. Searching, sorting or filtering often proves to work well in practice, because, for example, case number, reference number, client name etc. end up in all the documents anyway.

5. Have the records sent to a sub-folder in the document library in the records center by means of rules. We applied this solution in our workable demo. As indicated in *Chapter 5, Workable demo*, in the section *Configure the drop-off library*, this requires metadata fields that are mandatory and which are not of the text type. This method will therefore not offer an all-encompassing solution in all cases, but it may be combined with alternative 4.

Document sets

In the paper world, we all know the folder, which contains various documents. The folder keeps these documents together, physically and substantively as well: all documents from the folder are related to one another. A name, a file number or project code is usually written on the file, and perhaps other metadata as well, such as the date on which the folder was created and the name of the person handling the case, the name of the person (or company) that is the subject of the file and the type of file. After the introduction of SharePoint 2007, many customers requested Microsoft to look into the possibility of relating documents to one another in the same way. Microsoft granted this wish in SharePoint 2010 with the introduction of the document set. In view of the features above, the document set could meet the substantive, document-related requirements of case management.

I will not elaborate on the functional possibilities and features of document sets here: I will only focus on the aspect of records management. For more information on document sets see (1). In order to be able to follow the text, it is only important to know that:

- A document set itself is also a content type
- A document set may contain various types of documents, each with their own content type
- A document set has metadata
- The metadata of the document set may be adopted by the documents in the document set
- A document set may have versions. This is a layer on top of the versions of the individual documents, which may be regarded as a file status at a specific point in time

Document sets and in-place records management

It is not possible to apply in-place records management with document sets. This is because the document set is derived from the folder content type, and record declaration is not possible for this type.

Relocating the entire document set

Just like separate documents, document sets can be relocated to a records center. A peculiarity here is that the document sets are compressed and can also be viewed in their compressed state in the drop-off library. During dispatch to the final target library, they are extracted again as per usual. This fact probably received so much attention on the Internet because it takes much longer before the document sets are sent to their final destination, at least when they have the same priority. In this case, it looks as though a valid document set is compressed, sent to the drop-off library and never leaves there.

Organizing document sets in the records center

Just as with separate documents, rules may be used in the content organizer to distribute document sets over the document libraries that are present in the records center. It is also possible to send record sets to a different library, on the basis of the values from a metadata field. Figure 6.1 below provides an example of such a rule. Do ensure that the rule should specifies that all three values need to be selected. The document will not be sent to the specified document library if only one or two values are selected in the record metadata. Because these errors can easily be made and are difficult to trace at a later stage, it is important not to make the rules too complicated and to test them extensively. Various conditions may be created within a rule, which should all complied with, before a rule is launched. Three different rules will have to be created in order to ensure that all documents are added, for which the user role is electro-technical engineer, safety engineer or high pressure specialist.

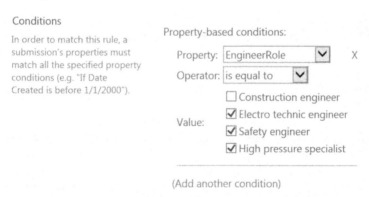

Figure 6.1: Rule for sending a record to a specific document library in the records center

It is not possible to create a folder within a document library on the basis of the properties of a metadata field. This functionality deviates from that of ordinary documents. Whether the option is available should depend on the type of metadata fields, which should be suitable to serve as a basis for the rules. Oddly, if a different content type is first selected – for which this option is actually displayed – and subsequently the correct content type, then the option is available. If the rules are subsequently filled in, stored and viewed again, the rules for creating folders appear to have disappeared. So it is not possible after all.

I do not really mind this where it concerns the organization of records. The document sets themselves are already a type of folder, and it is also possible to create views on the basis of the metadata. Yet this could lead to problems when a great many documents sets are sent to a library. New libraries will then have to be created manually or automatically when the library becomes unmanageably large. The best option, of course, is to try to assess the amount of records of a certain type in advance, and to configure suitable rules that neatly distribute the records over various document libraries.

Versions of document sets

As discussed, document sets may have versions that exist alongside the versions of the individual documents. The records center facilitates configuration for ordinary documents where a new version is created in the document library for every version that is sent to the records center. This is different for document sets, where the new version receives a name that consists of the original name, plus an addition of arbitrary letters, see Figure 6.2. This is even the case when you select in the content organizer settings that versioning should be used, and when this is enabled in the library version.

Figure 6.2: Naming versions of document sets in the records center

Microsoft was apparently unable to keep the behavior for document sets identical to that of ordinary documents. This is not really surprising when you realize that document sets are actually a type of folder.

Welcome page

As indicated, a document set has an introduction page that functions as the front page of the file. What is particularly useful is that the shared metadata can be displayed on the welcome page. In SharePoint, the page offers the option of placing all kinds of web parts on it, with which functionality is obtained. The welcome page is also preserved in the record center. Some sources on the Internet indicate the contrary, but perhaps this concerns older versions.

Adding documents to a document set at a later stage

It is not unusual that, after the case has been transferred to the records management system, a document should be added. Think of reopening a case, or adding a document that arrived late, without this influencing the case itself.

The reopening of a case creates an entirely new situation. This is why both the old and the new situation should be stored separately in the records center as sets of records (the document sets). The standard solution of SharePoint – the creation of a file with an adapted name – works perfectly here. It is also possible to archive the file under a new or adapted name.

Adding a document to an existing, archived document set is not automatically possible. The rules of the content organizer do not allow for this. In principle, it should be possible to add a new version alongside the old document set, to which the new documents are added. The old version could subsequently be optionally removed. This method would be permissible in an emergency, for example if the document set is checked and approved, but is incomplete on reflection. If the addition of documents occurs fairly routinely, and does not lead to an essentially different case status but would indeed involve the recording of a new status, this is a crude tool.

References

1. Microsoft. Introduction to document sets. https://support.office.com/en-ie/article/Introduction-to-Document-Sets-c49c246d-31f1-4bfe-afe2-e26698b47e05

Chapter 7

Management functions

Vital records

Vital records are records that are recognized as being essential for the company. It should be possible for these records to quickly create an overview of their location. Depending on the application, various options are possible:

- Define a content type *Vital record* and optionally derive any other content types from it for the various business processes. Create rules in the records center with which the vital records for every derived content type are sent to document libraries. This solution emphasizes the separate treatment of vital records. The fact that these records are essential is strongly emphasized in the various dimensions in which they may be classified. The vital records are separated from the other records in the process. They are physically grouped together in order to facilitate corresponding management of the vital records. For example, it is possible to create a separate back-up regime of the underlying database.
- Define a metadata field in the basic content type of the organization and ensure that this field is inherited in all underlying content types. Whenever a record is a vital record, this will be indicated in this field. It is also possible to define the field in such a way that it acquires a value of 1-5, for example, where 5 is a vital record. Because the records are now also fully part of the records belonging to a specific process, they will receive the same treatment as the other documents in the processes, ending up in various locations in the records center. Within the records center, it is possible to use a standard content search web part, enabling the various vital records to be displayed as desired.
- Use in-place records management as described in Chapter 5.

Overview of records of which the retention period will expire

In many cases, organizations wish to have an insight into the records for which the retention period will expire. This is not a standard functionality of SharePoint, but it may be partly realized by adding the standard metadata field *Expiration date*: this field indicates when the active rule from the retention policy of a document or record expires. It is again possible to use the content search web part (CSWP) in the records center in order to configure a search function that displays the records for which the expiration date lapses within a month, for example. Yet the CSWP is unable to see whether the rule that expires actually signifies the destruction of the document.

Another required functionality is starting a workflow with which the destruction of a record may be approved. It may be created relatively easily with SharePoint designer. This is a tool with which workflows may be created, among others. Whether this is a customization depends on the criteria used. Search on the Internet for more information using the search term *'expiration workflow SharePoint'*. When all records are subject to such a workflow, it is possible to insert a destruction date in the workflow, which enables the production of overviews by means of a CSWP.

Hierarchical file plan and content types

A file plan may be fully implemented within a SharePoint list. The various attributes in this list form the meta-metadata in this case. A SharePoint list is basically a flat table without a hierarchy. This hierarchy may still be created in the following two ways:

- By means of folders
- By applying grouping to the meta-metadata

Although folders have their application in SharePoint, the use of metadata is much more flexible. In fact, the flexibility of sorting, filtering and grouping on the basis of metadata is such that –when combined with the use of views – many tools fall by the wayside. Figure 7.1 shows a simplified example of a view on a file plan. Another view could be the content types that only relate to the North region, grouped by process and subsequently by phase. These views may be immediately selected in the list. In practice, you will often want to create a separate page where views focused on the task are displayed in a transparent manner, for example as part of a management dashboard for the file plan.

✔	Title	Content Type	Phase	Process group	Region
▷ **Region : East** (2)					
◢ **Region : North** (4)					
◢ Process group : HR (1)					
	E	•••	Execution	HR	North
◢ Process group : Primary (3)					
	Manual	••• ACTH Manual	Execution	Primary	North
	Biochemical Manual	••• ☐ ACTH Biochemical Manual CT	Execution	Primary	North
	D	•••	Preproject	Primary	North
▷ **Region : South** (1)					

Figure 7.1: Default view on the file plan, showing all items grouped by Region and then by process group.

In SharePoint, the content types are created and displayed in the user interface. A file plan can be (strongly) hierarchical. This is not supported in the standard user interface, in which it is possible to create groups with content types, but in which deeper levels are not possible. If the number of content types is in the order of hundreds, this will become somewhat cluttered. SharePoint has its limitations here. But it is possible to simulate a hierarchical ordering by providing content types with a prefix that corresponds with the higher level in the hierarchy of the file plan, the reason being that the groups and content types in a group are alphabetically ordered in the user interface. This may not be a very neat solution, but it may provide additional support for the two levels (group and content type within the group), which are standardly available. The displayed view is configured in the user interface of SharePoint itself. More advanced views may be created with the help of SharePoint designer or Access, which is integrated in SharePoint.

Scalability

In SharePoint 2007, the platform still had major limitations in relation to scalability. Document libraries, sites and site collections were very much limited in terms of size. In SharePoint 2013 Server and Office 365, these limitations have largely been eliminated. Multinationals with over 100,000 employees use SharePoint for all their unstructured data and phase out their old ECM platforms. As the SharePoint records management solution fits with the functionality of document libraries, sites and site collections, the greatly increased possibilities also apply in these areas. Good planning will then be necessary.

Level of records centers

So far, we have focused on a solution with only one records center. For larger organizations and certainly for multinationals, the storage capacity of a single records center will not be sufficient. They usually have various SharePoint farms in different parts of the world with various functions. In these cases, it is useful and necessary to divide the records over a number of records centers. This is an advanced scenario that, to my knowledge, has never been put into practice.

When several records centers are used, the rules may be implemented in a centralized or decentralized manner. In the first case, a single records center is responsible for recording and implementing the rules. In the event of decentralized implementation, certain document types are sent to one records center, and other document types to another. Every records center handles the routing of its own document types. This is actually the same configuration as in the workable demo, but then in plural.

The central routing of documents is arranged in the content organizer settings. This menu is available from the site settings in the records center. The option *Sending to Another Site* is specifically intended for records centers and other sites that threaten to become too large because of the enormous number of documents sent to them. With the help of rules for the drop-off library, documents can be sent to other site collections. Obviously, adapting existing rules is not something you are happy to do as an administrator, because of the additional workload and also because of the risk of errors. It is therefore important to factor in wide margins and growth in the design of the records center. The formal limit for the size of a site collection (the records center is technically a site collection) is 1 terabyte (TB) in 2015. Many organizations use smaller maximum values, for example 100 gigabyte (GB).

Site and document library level

Because a records center is largely based on a standard site collection, all the options for configuring it are also available. These include the creation of new sites and new document libraries within the site.

Folder Partitioning

Folder partitioning is configured in the **content organizer settings**. This relates to the size of folders within document libraries: SharePoint is only able to process up to 5,000 items in the same view. Again, companies often use lower maximum values; between 1,000 and 2,000 items. In this context, it is also wise to give careful consideration in advance, and to immediately distribute the records over folder or document libraries on the basis of rules. This gives the administrator more control than in the case of automatic partitioning.

Duplicate entries and versions

The configuration that relates to the situation in which a record already occurs under the same name in the target location (a document library or a folder within a document library) is also configured in the **Content organizer settings**. In this case, it is possible to add a SharePoint version to the same document, or to create a new file, in which case a number of arbitrary letters are added to the name. If various versions are added under the same name, and these are also part of the same phase in the business process, then the versions are very suitable. If the various versions belong to a different phase in the business process, and it is important to clearly reflect this, the method of automatic re-naming is to be preferred.

Auditing

If auditing is specified at the source location of the document, the audit data for the document may be included for the records library. In addition, the metadata information is included, and this is something you will certainly want. This value should remain as a default, and should therefore be checked.

Enforcing records management

For document libraries for which rules are specified in the drop-off library, mandatory use of the drop-off library may be enforced, so that documents cannot be uploaded directly. In this case, use the option *Redirect Users to the Drop-Off Library* in the **Content organizer settings.** This option applies to the document libraries for which rules are specified in the drop-off library. In the records center, this involves all document libraries, but for other sites that use a drop-off library this does not need to be the case. If this option is selected, users can no longer send their documents to libraries through uploading, but only by means of the drop-off library. If they try to do so anyway, they will see the screen below, see Figure 7.2. Their upload to the document library is automatically converted into an upload to the drop-off library. This makes the use of these document libraries more formal, and it prevents users from sending documents to this library in an 'underhand' way. This is useful for the document libraries in the record center and also for the knowledge library in the workable demo of A-Works, for example. The documents that are located there should be formally approved, as agreed. It would be very risky if users were able to upload their own manual, possibly resulting in engineers following the wrong manual. Many companies also have knowledge libraries where all staff members are allowed to add their own documents, when they think that they may be usefully re-used. In this case, you would not want to implement the rule.

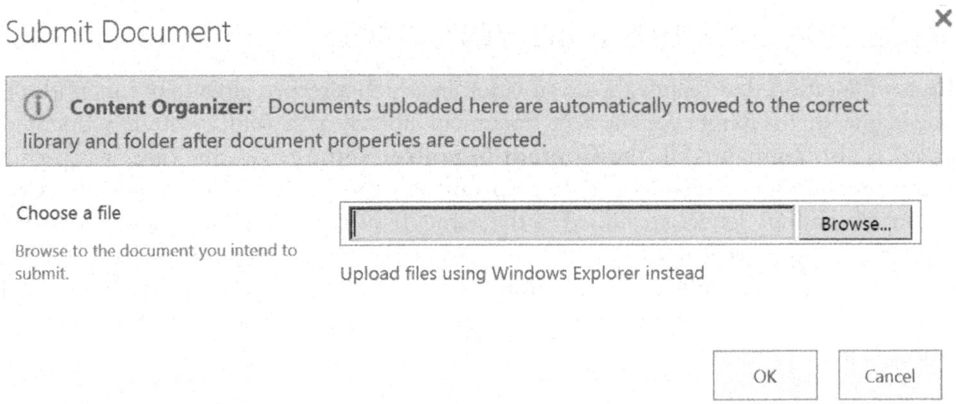

Submit Document   ✕

ⓘ **Content Organizer:** Documents uploaded here are automatically moved to the correct
library and folder after document properties are collected.

Choose a file | Browse... |

Browse to the document you intend to
submit.   Upload files using Windows Explorer instead

                                                    | OK | | Cancel |

Figure 7.2: Notification screen when sending a document directly to the records center

Chapter 8

Metadata and Taxonomy

The canonical definition of metadata is: data that describes other data. This is shown in Figure 8.1, where you see that elementary facts, data, are transformed into information by adding an interpretation or meaning. Data in itself has little value: the number 14.735.722 for example has no intrinsic meaning. When you know, however, that 14.735.722 is the profit of your company last year and that the currency is Euro, this becomes information.

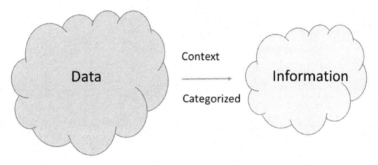

Figure 8.1: Data and information

So metadata provides context to data, or makes it possible to categorize it. See Figure 8.1. This is precisely what makes data into information. Interestingly, there is no such thing as *the* context for any given piece of data or information. It may be seen from multiple perspectives by different user groups.

In the ISO standard 15489 (1) on records management, metadata is defined as data describing the context, content and structure of records and their management through time. This is a more precise definition, which is only applicable to the narrower scope of records management. In this chapter, the broader, more general uses are also given.

Why you need metadata

In this section we will discuss metadata by looking at the use cases for document management and from thereon look at what is needed in terms of metadata. In this way we make metadata a first class citizen.

Metadata is important in the following areas:

- Collaboration
- Business processes

- Management of documents
- Records management

Collaboration

After the initial version of a document has been created, people start working on it together. This process is known as collaboration (although collaboration has also a much broader meaning). When collaborating in the classical ways, using file shares or e-mail, some problems arise, such as:

- Documents cannot be found in the folder hierarchy or mail
- Multiple versions of documents exist in different places or in mail and it is not clear which is the latest
- Information from previous versions is lost
- It is not clear who edited which section of the document
- The folders require a great deal of management
- It is difficult to find documents
- There is a very limited audit trail
- Collaboration with people outside the company, such as suppliers and customers, is cumbersome
- As a consequence of the previous points, authenticity, integrity and reliability are not ensured

Collaboration in SharePoint solves these issues by leveraging the power of metadata, and a great deal of useful metadata is supplied out-of-the-box:

- Status: this may be the status of a workflow such as the out-of-the-box approval workflow, or a custom status field. This is important because the actions that are permitted depend on their status. Editing for instance will not be allowed when the document is final. Review only makes sense when it has been offered for review et cetera
- Ownership: in many cases, the original creator of a document can be regarded as the owner. This is not always the case, however. Formal ownership of documents in a document library can also belong to the head of the business unit or the knowledge manager. The owner is responsible for the quality of the document and only the owner can decide whether a document can be removed.
- Version history: this is not shown as a column (it would not fit) but it is accessed from a dropdown menu. The version history can provide very important context to a document, for instance when it is not clear who added, changed or removed a certain section.
- Checked out to: if you use check in/check out, this gives you the opportunity to contact the person who checked out the document if you need to make changes yourself.
- Edited date/edited by: gives you information on who made the latest edits on the document

Business processes

Metadata may be used to support business processes. The typical approach to this is to organize workshops and interviews and have key users state what metadata they think would be useful. Since the output of this was often disappointing, I decided to do it in reverse. Instead of specifying the metadata, users are asked what actions they perform on their documents in the context of a process. I then help users decide which metadata they need to support these actions and processes. This way, we obtain results that are more relevant. There are less metadata that have no actual use after all and the needs of the users are better supported.

During the elicitation process you will run into a challenge called tacit knowledge, which is 'knowledge in the head' that is hard to express in words, since the owner is not actually aware of it (anymore). They are not aware of the everyday routine just like you don't have to think about your way from home to the office. It is quite amazing that you can sit in your car, listen to the radio, think of all the things you think about, barely having to make conscious decisions on which turn to take, only to find out after half an hour that you have arrived.

The common approach for eliciting tacit knowledge is to interview multiple people, compare results and come back with detailed questions. After a while the analyst knows enough about the process to elicit new actions. Bringing people together in a workshop or brainstorming sessions is also a common practice. Another approach is to create a workable demo (or working example or proof of concept). This has the advantage that your users can actually see what you have created and this will spark their ideas. If you have relevant data in your working example, users may actually gain some hands-on experience. That is where tacit knowledge surfaces immediately. You will obtain comments such as: "This is not practical: I get too many results. I usually filter on role." Then you know you need to have *Role* as a metadata field.

Business processes are specific to the organization and SharePoint cannot have generic metadata fields for this. Fortunately, a lot of these specific user actions have a common background:

- Searching & finding: this is using standard SharePoint search to find documents or list items, also called full text search. In some cases however, using keywords can narrow down the number of search results dramatically, making the remaining results much more relevant. If you have ever performed an Internet search on the subject of *e-mail*, you will have encountered the problem that, next to the items you search, a large number of results which just have an e-mail address somewhere in the text are given. The general case is when you have a specific term on which to filter that happens to be a very common general term in your organization as well. Using SharePoint managed metadata is the solution. This is elaborated on in the Workable demo, chapter 5.
- Sorting & filtering: SharePoint search helps you a great deal when you have no idea where to look, especially since FAST became the standard search engine in SharePoint 2013. However, document usage follows the 90-10 rule, where 90% of the document usage of a given document can be attributed to a small number

of key users (10% or more likely even less). For these users, using general search to find documents is not efficient, as they know where to find the information. They just need help in arriving quickly at the right document. Metadata for sorting and filtering provides exactly that. The regular users know in which document library the document resides, they just need a quick sort or filter that shows it on top of all the other documents.

- Context: as we have seen in the introduction, providing context is the general, overarching use of metadata. More specifically, in the area of business processes, context is often required as it determines the interpretation of the document or the operations that are valid. Now we are going to extend the workable demo from the previous chapters a little. Let us say that the manuals we have seen have a *Source* metadata field, which can be internal (created within the company itself, by a colleague) or external (created by the manufacturer). When a procedure is not correct for an in-company document, the owner of the document should be contacted. The company could be liable for any damage as a result of not adhering to the manual. When an operational procedure mentioned in a document appears not to be fully correct in a manufacturer document, the manufacturer should be contacted. Since thousands of people in the world work with the manual, there is only a slight chance that there are big mistakes in the manual. So both the interpretation of the contents and the actions that are valid depend on the *Source* metadata field.

- Ownership: many actions eventually lead to the owner of a document. This can be the creator, but this is not always the case. In a knowledge management system for instance, people may leave the business unit or the company for whatever reason, but users should still be able to contact the responsible person. Operations that typically require the involvement of the owner are: delete, change, move, merge and quality queries.

- Classify: classification is a very broad term. In the area of business processes it is used to group list items or documents together on certain criteria so they can be processed. This processing may be machine-based or it may be performed by human interaction.

- Status: during their lifecycle in SharePoint, documents will have a document based status as mentioned in the section on collaboration. In some cases, documents may also have a process-specific status. The document may be created as one step in a larger process. For each phase in the status, a number of actions may be allowed, by a limited set of roles. Or the document may be based on external documentation (legislation for example) which provides a higher-order status. The internal status must then map with the status that is in use externally.

Management of documents

Often overlooked in the analysis process is metadata related to management of the documents. Managing the information essentially boils down to making sure the user can quickly find relevant information. This means that the quality of the material should be kept high, which in turn means that irrelevant or obsolete information should be removed or made recognizable as such. In general, the functional administrator who manages the solution does not decide whether information is old, but metadata can provide a strong clue. The administrator can then notify the owner that the document should be reviewed. Many of the metadata fields required for management are generated by SharePoint by default. They just need to be included in a management view.

Some useful metadata fields are:

- Status: the status of the document may give an indication on what to do with a document. A document that has been in draft for a year is probably not used.
- Size and data type: these give a general indication of the nature of the document
- Date of creation and date of last change: these give a general indication on the life cycle of the document but may also be used for more formal review- or withdrawal policies. The stages for retention policies may be based on the creation date or the date of last change.
- Ownership: the owner decides on what actions are allowed for their documents. They may have delegated ownership to other persons however, including the creator of the document or the functional administrator. In case of doubt, it is always the owner who decides. The owner is also held responsible for the quality of the documents.

Records management

Traditionally, records management is one of the areas that has most closely been associated with the use of metadata. This is the consequence of the fact that records are taken out of the day-to-day process in which they were used. The document should be understandable to a general user at a later time. This can only be achieved by capturing the context of the document. Metadata is also important in records management because formal policies are driven by metadata. Important aspects of records management supported by metadata are:

- Findability (efficient retrieval): storing records is of little use if they cannot be found later. The ISO 23081 standard (2) pays special attention to finding related documents by their metadata.
- Reliability: metadata can be used to show how documents or list items have been used through time, how they were stored and which life cycle they have gone through. All this information adds to the reliability of the information asset.
- Authenticity: a document must be genuine in the sense that it must be indisputable who has created the document, when it was created and in cooperation with whom.
- Readability (interoperability): records may be retained over very long periods, especially if they are part of the cultural heritage of a nation. Encodings may become obsolete over such a long time. Metadata can help in specifying technical data ensuring that the information remains readable over time.
- Context: metadata can help put documents in their business context. This process-specific context helps interpreting the text correctly.

- Applying archiving rules: records will be archived automatically according to the rules set

Metadata in SharePoint: content types and columns

Content Types are the way SharePoint deals with document types. A Content Type has Columns that provide metadata fields, placeholders for the metadata. Each document of a given Content Type can have different values for each metadata field. This is the metadata of the document.

The same mechanism is used for Lists, which can also be based on Content Types. As with document libraries, the values for each entry will be shown in their column in the list. Although the SharePoint document library is just a type of list, conceptually they are completely different. Lists are lightweight tables and fall into the category of structured data. Document libraries are containers for documents, being unstructured data. For documents, the extra columns in the document library are metadata, they provide additional context to the document. For lists, each item is a row in the table, made up of all the values on the different columns. So strictly speaking, columns in a document library provide metadata and columns in a list do not. List data is referred to as metadata by some, however.

If you create a site content type at the root site of a site collection, that site content type becomes available on any site below it in the site hierarchy. If you add a new content type to a site that is lower down in the hierarchy, it is available on the site where you add it and on any sites below that site in the hierarchy.

To complicate matters, lists and libraries have their own columns. You can create them directly on the list or library, or you can add a content type, by which you copy the columns of the content type to the list. When, at a later stage, you change the content type, you will be asked if you want to change dependent content types. This refers to the lists or libraries that copied columns from that content type (it also copies the changes to content types that you derived from the original content type).

So there are two ways to create metadata columns in your library (or list):

- Adding the columns directly
- Adding a content type, which brings over all the columns defined in the content type

I would advise you to use the second method, although you might be tempted to use the first, as it is lean and mean. As with most quick solutions, however, things get messy rather quickly. If you have two types of documents you want to store in a document library, for example, you will have two sets of columns. After some time you will probably see that:

- Columns may have different names but are essentially the same (you typically only discover this after you entered metadata for a number of documents in both libraries)

- Columns have the same name, but when you try to merge the libraries at a later stage, you will face one (or more) of the following challenges:

    o the range of valid values is different

    o one column is free text and the other has a limited set of values

    o the allowed length of the text is different

    o the allowed range for numbers is different

    o other subtle differences between the columns

Would you not have had these problems if you had defined content types? If you create content types without any planning, you may encounter similar problems. The great advantage of content types, however, is that you are forced to think carefully about what you do.

If you have multiple document libraries or lists for the same content type, you can simply add the content type to each list and all columns will be created. Even if you pay careful attention and create exactly the same columns in the list by hand, you have a problem when you want to change metadata in a later stage. You then have to delete, add or change the column manually. When you have a centrally defined content type, you can change it in one place. In other words: content types allow for more manageable solutions. They follow the more general design principle: *Define and manage in one place, use everywhere.*

In SharePoint 2007, you could only apply metadata at the document and list item levels. In SharePoint 2010, document sets were introduced, allowing you to specify metadata relevant to a group of documents. The documents in the dataset can have their own metadata as well as inheriting metadata from the document set.

Another feature introduced in SharePoint 2010 and continued in SharePoint 2013 is Location based metadata. It allows for setting defaults for metadata on the document library or folders within a document library. These defaults are applied when you upload a single file or when you upload multiple files at once. This has become the main use of location based metadata as it helps alleviate one of the most gruesome tasks in older versions of SharePoint: adding metadata when copying from the file system to SharePoint.

In a common scenario, documents on the file system have to be transferred to a newly created document library. Before location based metadata, the options were to enter the metadata manually for each and every document or to let all documents have the same metadata. Location based metadata allows you to specify metadata defaults per folder in the document library. Users can drag their files to the suitable folder and the right metadata is added. After all users have finished copying, you can either have a view not showing the folders, or you can do some extra work to remove the folders while keeping documents and metadata. There are of course limitations to this approach: if you have ten valid values for a column this requires ten folders. For multiple folders, you would see a combinatorial explosion, requiring hundreds of different folders if you want to deal with all combinations. In many cases however, a limited number of folders can save your users 80-90% of the work.

Location based metada defaults is a nice name for just giving defaults to column values in a document library or list. To do this, perform the following steps:

1. In the Library tab of your document library, select Library settings
2. Under General settings, select Column default value settings
3. You can now set defaults for each column that support setting of default values by selecting them, as shown in Figure 8.2

Note that for Choice, columns, like the ones shown in the figure below, you cannot select one of the choices, you have to remember them exactly as they are spelled. There is something left to improve here.

Settings ▸ Change Default Column Values ⓘ

Column (click to edit default value)	Type	Default Value	Source of Default Value	Used In
EngineerRole	Choice		Document Library	BTCH Manual, BCTH Biochemcial Manual
EquipmentType	Choice		Document Library	BTCH Manual, BCTH Biochemcial Manual
InstallationType	Choice	Medical	Document Library	BTCH Manual, BCTH Biochemcial Manual

Figure 8.2: Setting default values for the columns in a document library

You can select default values on the document library level, or for each folder below it, using the same menu.

Metadata structure

The metadata challenge is not restricted to a single document type or even a number of separate document types. In practice you will have a number of document types that are related to each other and that also have related metadata. To complicate matters further, there might be a metadata scheme at company or business unit level to which you must adhere, but which does not quite suit your needs. You need a metadata structure to address all design choices and present your users with good quality metadata from the start. I do not use the term metadata schema myself in the SharePoint context, as it is used in a more formal way, addressing issues such as common semantics, the use of namespaces et cetera. While important, SharePoint offers us a framework to use, in which all relevant aspects are solved for us.

In ISO 23081 and governmental documentation there is a strong tendency to focus on the formal aspects of metadata. This is a logical consequence of striving towards a consistent and broadly applicable system. The focus is also on using metadata in the context of records management. Within the context of a company, it is difficult if not impossible to realize a metadata scheme that fits all. Each business unit has its own needs and users do not like to fill in metadata for which they do not see a purpose. Searching, filtering, sorting and status are important in business processes and metadata specific to the business unit is often required to make this possible. The finance department for example would want to add metadata from the financial viewpoint and HR from the human resources perspective.

The picture that emerges from this is to have tight control on metadata at the organizational level and more freedom when the number of users falls lower and the mode of operation is more specific. Both sides have their own criteria: standardization, re-use and universal interpretation versus flexibility and usability in a specific context. The importance of flexibility and usability is often underestimated by metadata purists, causing annoyance for users. By using the approach described in the section *Business processes* you can prevent this.

Some metadata can be generated automatically from the system context, such as author and date, or can be inherited from the Office document. See the *section Automatically generating metadata from Word*. All other metadata need to be entered by the users. In practice people tend to strongly dislike entering metadata. If the metadata is complex or the benefits are not clear to the user, they will not add metadata or will not do it in a consistent way. So this 'excessive' metadata should either be generated automatically or removed. In this way, only simple systems remain, which will save you a lot of trouble. In my day-to-day practice, I see too many metadata systems which are too complicated. In the end, these become chaotic and are worse than having no metadata at all.

To summarize, strongly different needs exist for metadata within the company and there is no one-size-fits-all approach. What we need is a hierarchical system in which more specific document types inherit metadata from global document types, while adding metadata that makes them specific. SharePoint content types provide this functionality, in which inheritances enables classes of documents to share characteristics across an organization, and it enables teams to customize these characteristics for their specific needs. So the higher the content type is in the hierarchy, the less metadata (site columns) it has, because less metadata is relevant for each and every team in the organization. The lower the content type is in the hierarchy, the more metadata it has, because for each specific level, extra details are added. At the top level are the SharePoint standard content types such as document, (list) item and page. In Figure 8.3 below, an example is given of such a hierarchy for a subset of customer related documents in a bank. An important point to note is that the arrows indicate a so-called is-a relationship. So an Article is-a Document and both Research and News are both Articles, et cetera.

Users should pick the relevant document type for their document as it contains all relevant metadata. Since the hierarchy consists of an is-a relationship, taking a document type higher in the hierarchy is also valid but less specific, so a great deal of information is lost. In practice, the fact that users will have to add less metadata may be a reason for a significant group to use say, the Document type instead of the One Pager. The is-a relationship is often not completely understood, so some people may pick any document type on a hierarchical line (Document – Article – Research - Fact Sheet, for example). You can help yourself and your users by allowing only the document types that are really in a document library. In most cases this will only be the leaf nodes[1], the lowest document type in each hierarchical line you can make. For the hierarchy presented in Figure 8.3 the leaf nodes are Stock Research, Fact Sheet, One Pager and News.

SharePoint uses content types to implement such a hierarchy. The topmost item is always a standard SharePoint content type which cannot be changed. Your content type can use this as its parent. Building a hierarchy in this way is quite easy. The most difficult part is to get your information analysis straight.

1

     The term *leaf* comes from mathematical graph theory. When turned upside down, the figure resembles a tree, with the lowest block being the *root* of the tree and all top most blocks being *leaves*. A mathematically better way to put this is to say that a *root* has no parent and a *leaf* has no children.

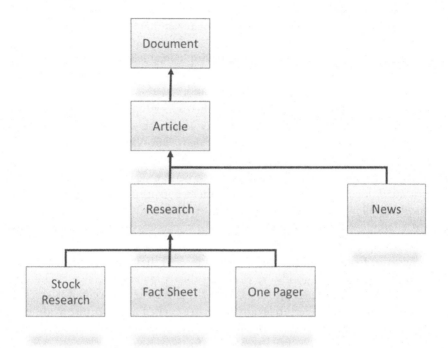

Figure 8.3: Hierarchy of document types for a bank.

Metadata at the organization level

An important step in metadata design is determining what metadata is needed for all documents and what metadata is needed at the business unit level, such as HR, Finance or Sales. If you skip this step you might run in one of these two situations:

- Important organization-wide metadata does not get incorporated into groups of documents. It might be determined, for example, that the security level of the document is an obligatory metadata field for all documents in the organization. If this is the case, a column should be added to the content type that enforces this. If not, some business levels may choose not to add it to the metadata at their level, leaving the security levels of their documents unclear.
- Organization-wide metadata gets named differently for different groups of documents. So the metadata field from the example above may be named Security level in the HR department, SL (Security Level) in the IT department and have other names in other departments as well, making it hard for the users to understand the metadata from documents originating in other departments. It also makes it much harder to produce analytics on say, the location of highly secure documents.

There is of course a balance between capturing anything that might be useful in metadata (and creating a burden for users) and not capturing metadata (not supporting users, records management and information management).

Some fields that I think might be useful at the organizational level:

- Language. In an organization where multiple languages are used for documents, this is an important filter for relevant documents as you typically only want documents in the languages you understand.
- Business unit. The business unit gives the ownership at the highest level for the document. Over the years, people may leave the company, organizations are restructured and documents are migrated. The Business unit then at least provides some clue to the origins of the document.
- Security classification. It is important that people realize they are working with a classified document. From the management perspective, having the security level specified allows for automated checks or reports, in which risks can be traced. An example of this is the occurrence of a classified document in a document library that is open to anyone.
- Whatever fields you choose, make sure you have a sound motivation for introducing them. A good way of doing this is making use cases. The examples above give a (very general) use case for the three fields specified. Use cases help ensure that only the very relevant fields are picked as enterprise wide metadata. Make it easier for yourself by having the metadata field and their use cases challenged by managers, key users and information architects.

There is more metadata that is generally useful to the organization. In fact, the following fields are so common that they are provided by SharePoint as standard fields, as shown in Table 8.1:

Metadata field	Use	Automatic
Title	Identification of document, findability	From Office document
Created By	From Office	From Office document
Changed By	Findability co-author	From Office document
Date created	Relevancy. Retention and disposition	From Office document
Date changed	Relevancy. Retention and disposition	From Office document
DocumentID	Identification document, tracking	Generated within SharePoint

Table 8.1: SharePoint standard metadata fields

Making your metadata solution user-friendly

Template based transfer

Fortunately, it is also possible to have your own metadata fields synchronized between SharePoint and Word. The way to do this is to make the link between Word and SharePoint in a Word template. The fields belonging to the content type are coupled to Quick part fields in Word. This is also why this method doesn't work for Excel, as it has no Quick parts. You can place the Quick parts anywhere in your document. In this way you have a smooth alignment with your template. For the transfer of standard metadata from the previous section, I remarked that to users, it still feels as though they need extra time to fill in the metadata. The strange thing is that when the same metadata is part of a template, users seem much more motivated to fill in the same fields. This came as a surprise to me, as I can find no real reason for it. The behavior is fairly consistent, however. You will probably have noted that most people fill in all fields in a template, even if it is not applicable in a given situation. For documents and metadata, one of the reasons why template-based metadata works better is that it is filled in beforehand. Some people have the idea that they have not properly begun until they have entered the first (template-based) page of the document, while metadata is commonly added afterward (the document information panel changes this somewhat).

Since this is a feature that helps alleviate the metadata burden where it hurts most and not many people know it, I will describe how it can be done in the hands-on section below.

1 Create Word template

Create a Word document suitable for the document type and save it locally as a template (.dotx). At this point you do not yet add the fields for metadata mapping

2 Create content type

Create the content type based on one of the document types from your information analysis. Add the right metadata columns. For content types, you can specify the template you created in step 1. You will find this below **Advanced settings**, see Figure 8.4.

Site Content Type ▸ Advanced Settings ⓘ

Document Template

Specify the document template for this content type.

⦿ Enter the URL of an existing document template:

> A-Works classified document

◯ Upload a new document template:

> | Browse... |

Read Only

Choose whether the content type is modifiable. This setting can be changed later from this page by anyone with permissions to edit this type.

Should this content type be read only?

◯ Yes
⦿ No

Update Sites and Lists

Specify whether all child site and list content types using this type should be updated with the settings on this page. This operation can take a long time, and any customizations made to the child site and list content types will be lost.

Update all content types inheriting from this type?

⦿ Yes
◯ No

Figure 8.4: Advanced settings for template-based transfer

3 Add Content Type

Go to the document library where you want the document type to reside. In the document library, if you have not already done so, allow for the management of content types in advanced settings. On the library settings, click **Add from existing content types** and select your content type from step 1.

4 Add the fields to the template and attach again to the content type

Create a document based on your template by going to the **Files** tab, selecting **New document** in your document library and then the content type you just added, see Figure 8.5. The document will open.

Figure 8.5: Opening a word document based on the specified template

In the document, go to the **Insert** tab on the ribbon, select **Quick parts** and then **Document property**. Select the right property, see Figure 8.6. You can drag the field to any place in the Word document you like. Typical places are the front page of the document and header and footer sections. Try to comply with the existing document layout. Save the document as a template (.dotx) again. Attach the template to the document type again, like you did in step 1.

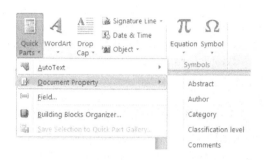

Figure 8.6: Adding a quickpart.

Tool based metadata extraction

Numerous tools are available that claim to extract metadata out of Word (or other) documents. Some are capable of adding them automatically to the appropriate SharePoint column. The capabilities offered by the tools are quite diverse. Some look at document properties, thus extracting standard document related metadata, others use artificial intelligence to extract the data.

At this point in time, tool based metadata extraction cannot replace manual metadata entry. It can provide valuable extra metadata though. Using one of these tools will certainly be very valuable if metadata is not available at all, for instance in the event of a previous migration of documents from a legacy system.

Some practical advice on metadata

The National Information Standards Organization (NISO) advices minimizing the use of free text fields (3). Translated to the SharePoint universe, this is about the use of the Single line of text and the Multiple lines of text site columns. In SharePoint, these columns types allow you freedom, which you can often put to good use. Using Multiple lines in combination with the Enhanced rich text option is especially powerful. Such use is not about metadata, however, but actual data. In a list, for example, you can have a rich text field with the main information and other fields which are metadata (you see the distinction between data and metadata gets blurred in lists). What NISO refers to is the use of these fields as actual metadata, such as a description field used for giving extra information about a document. In some cases this can be valuable, but as NISO points out, there are a number of drawbacks to using free text, including:

- Variation in spelling
- Variation in use of abbreviations, formats for dates, et cetera
- Users may avoid filling out other elements, and instead put unstructured information into free text fields

Any of these may decrease the benefits of metadata. This is not only a theoretical consideration, I often see it happen in practice. The simple reason for this is that when a content type is created without enough consideration, the person creating the content type has no clear idea what values are valid for the site column. The quick solution to this is to allow for free text and hope for the best.

Taxonomies and controlled vocabularies

A taxonomy is, in its broadest sense, a classification. The canonical example is the biological ordering of all living beings. As an example, the Lion's *species* name is Panthera Leo. Its close relatives are the Tiger and the Jaguar and together they form the *Genus* Panthera. All members belong to the *Family* of Felidae or cats, which in turn belong to the *Order* of Carnivores. All Carnivores belong to the *Class* of Mammals.

The biological taxonomy forms a logical ordering of all living beings (as far as we know). It uses an *Is-a* relationship. To give another example: a table *Is-a* piece of furniture which *Is-an* artifact. This is one of two most fundamental grouping relationships. The other relation type is the *Has-a* relationship. A car Has-an engine which *Has-a* combustion chamber. Both relation types can be used to build a taxonomy.

Every organization uses a vast number of taxonomies, knowingly or unknowingly. These range from the products they make, the departments in the organization, locations, types of customers, legislation et cetera. As you can see, the taxonomies touch just about everything that is important in the organization.

Now in the science of taxonomy, classification is the goal. Within the organization and within the context of enterprise content management and metadata, classification is used to support the ECM functions such as findability and records management. Since taxonomies reflect the inner workings of the organization, they are very valuable for the classification of documents.

A related concept is that of the controlled vocabulary or metadata vocabulary. These are just lists of things, with no ordering. They have no multiple levels, which is a main characteristic of a taxonomy. In SharePoint, managed metadata has some characteristics of taxonomies and some of controlled vocabularies. It would not be very useful to create a hierarchy with many levels and a few items per level in SharePoint applications. Most metadata is flat, occasionally with a few levels.

SharePoint terminology

The *term store* is the place where SharePoint taxonomies are stored. Taxonomies are also referred to as managed metadata. As so often in SharePoint land, the concepts are used interchangeably.

The *term store management tool* is the interface you use to create and maintain the taxonomies. The term store and terms store management tool are often used interchangeably.

A *term set* is a group of terms. You could also see each term set, with the term sets and terms below it, as a separate taxonomy. In practice, you often specify that a column must contain a term from a specific term set.

A *term* is an item in a term set, consisting of a word or phrase. In taxonomy science, each term would be an entity, but within SharePoint, it may be any word or phrase. A term may contain other terms.

A *term group* is a collection of term sets.

Local term sets are created within the context of a site collection. They are not visible for users outside the scope of the site collection.

Global term sets are created outside the context of a site collection. They are visible enterprise wide.

Enterprise keywords are stored in a single term set that has no hierarchical ordering. It contains all the loose terms that users have found to be relevant, without bringing any order to them.

As you can see, Microsoft does not use the term taxonomy and the formal concepts. There is a good reason for this. Taxonomy is a science, completely dedicated to ordering each item in the correct position in the classification hierarchy. Moving a bird, for example, to another family in biological taxonomy is only done after years of careful consideration and discussion. SharePoint managed metadata is not about formal hierarchies. Its purpose is to create metadata of higher quality and better manageability. This may take some discussion, but in an organizational setting, the benefits of such a discussion should outweigh the costs. This means that the taxonomy should be very practical. This is precisely what Microsoft facilitates by using multiple term sets, which can be seen as little taxonomies on their own. For some people it is difficult to let loose the idea of a grand all-encompassing organization taxonomy. Before you start with the taxonomy, make sure everybody embraces the concept of a simple, practical taxonomy.

The relationship between metadata, metadata columns and managed metadata

Simply put, the terms in the term store hold the valid values for metadata columns belonging to content types (or lists). The relationship between the concepts is depicted in

Figure 8.7 Managed metadata is defined once in term sets and terms. Metadata columns can be seen as placeholders for managed metadata in the context of a content type or list. It is no requirement that metadata must be based on managed metadata, however. Each individual item has its own metadata, which is based on the values provided by managed metadata. The term store consists of Term sets (only one is shown in Figure 8.7 which all have a set of terms. Content types contain columns. Each column may be based on managed metadata or not. In Figure 8.7 the dark column is based on a term set in the term store. The content type is added to the list, which is reflected by the list columns, which now are copies of the content type columns. Since the dark column in the content type points to the term set, each individual item in the list must have a value in the dark column that is a term in the term set.

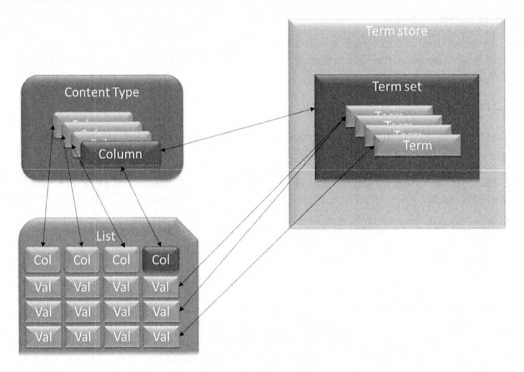

Figure 8.7. The relationship between metadata and taxonomy concepts. In the term store, a term set is defined consisting of 4 terms. The content type has one metadata field (column) which has managed metadata as its type. It is configured to point to the term set. In the list, the columns of the content type are inherited and so is the column that has the managed metadata type. Each row in the list is a unique entity, having its own value for each column. Two rows have the first term specified as its value, one row has the last term specified as its value.

Introducing or extending term sets in your organization

It is far from easy to create logical term sets that most people in your organization are willing to use. When you try to do this on your own, you are guaranteed to fail. It is a great deal of work and on your own you will never be able to get it done. Even if you could handle the amount of work, there are few persons in an organization having enough knowledge to create all term sets and terms. Another point to note is that the people actually using the terms will have a strong opinion on how these should be arranged. They will not use the term set if they think it matches poorly with reality.

The best way forward is to involve people who are knowledgeable in their own business area and have them design their own taxonomies. Now this takes some careful planning. Because the taxonomies touch many aspects of your organization, you would potentially need everyone. And this might overrun you budget. Another problem is that when you involve everyone at once, they will come up with partially overlapping term sets. The devil is always in the *partial*. If they were to overlap neatly you could unify them, but this seldom happens. Partially overlapping lists are based on partially overlapping criteria (that have of course not been made explicit), making it very hard to merge them.

To avoid confusion and excessive time expenditure you will have to use a hierarchical approach. First you will need to have term sets at enterprise and division levels. The high level organizational chart is an example of this. You can then involve middle managers, business analysts or other suitable roles for cooperation, providing the term sets at enterprise level. This way, all units will share a common basis. There is another advantage to this approach. One of the challenges in taxonomies is keeping them correct when the organization and the business change. Using the hierarchical approach helps you find the right owner for term sets. In practice, owners of a term set are not necessarily those who do the actual maintenance. At the higher organizational levels in particular, this responsibility will be delegated.

SharePoint 2013 allows each hierarchical level in the taxonomy to have its owner. These are the persons that actually perform the maintenance of the term set. This may work very well if the owners:

- Have the formal authority to maintain the term set (they have been given a mandate by the appropriate manager)
- Represent the user group
- Have the knowledge to decide on terms in the term set
- Have knowledge of SharePoint taxonomies

Some practical advice on terms and term sets

In the previous section I described a hierarchical approach to creating a taxonomy that is indeed useful in your organization. It is important however to understand that this does not mean you should involve many persons in the creation of your term sets and terms. Nor does it mean you should invest a lot of time in creating the taxonomy or take a long time to do so. Since the quality of your taxonomy should be high, this means that you cannot go deep and you cannot go broad. Keep things lean! Complex taxonomies are hard to create, hard to maintain and difficult to use.

Terms and term sets allow you to fill in a description. Often, these are left blank or the descriptions are trivial. In both cases they have little value. Instead, think as the user, having to choose between terms: *who are the users needing the term set and how can you help them choose the right term*. For instance, when an engineer has to fill in the equipment type that is required for a given type of installation, he might be tempted to create a really long list of all equipment that could possibly be needed. Since most equipment is on board the vans the engineers use when they go on a site visit, this would be quite useless. If you know this, create a description to make the engineer understand that only special equipment, which is not on the van's standard inventory, needs to be listed. On all levels of the taxonomy, descriptions can be made much better by taking the perspective of the user.

For a term, you can specify synonyms, using **Other labels** on the **General** Tab. These will be shown when a user types in the first few letters of the label. This may help you in finding quick solutions on different terms that are used between business units or even between people. It will also help you to flatten out the use of additional labels, since only the default labels are shown when entered.

Taxonomy management

Creating the first version of the taxonomy is one thing, but managing the taxonomy is something completely different. It is inevitable that changes to the taxonomy will have to be made, no matter how much effort you put in creating a stable first version. Changes in terms and term sets will arise as a consequence of changes in the organization, customers, environment, and simply because actually using the taxonomy brings new insights. The term store management tool provides several options to change terms and term sets such as copying, moving, re-using and pinning.

Renaming, moving or adding terms (or term sets) are relatively simple changes. It becomes more complicated when term sets have to be merged. This scenario typically occurs when two units have been employing different term sets for what is essentially the same thing. But there are more scenarios in which you need to merge terms. Merging the terms themselves is the easiest part of the change. The changes have no effect on the metadata in the document libraries, however. There is no standard functionality that lets you do this, as each case is unique. It can be automated with custom coding, however.

If your needs are not matched by the capabilities of the term store management tools, you can also look at third-party tools. At the time of writing, each tool seems to have its own specific feature, so you will buy a tool more for handling a specific task then to professionalize taxonomy management as a whole.

Tagging & Enterprise keywords

We have seen that managed metadata provides organizations with a way to control the quality of the metadata. We have also seen that creating and maintaining a taxonomy can be difficult and time consuming. The using of tagging and keywords provides an altogether different approach. Instead of going formal, it leaves the users free to create their tags. Because users may have a different view on the document than the creator, the tags will better match the expectations of other users. When many users tag a document, the most predominant tags will go on top.

To let users add keywords, you can add the enterprise keywords column to a list or document library. Users can then select the item and enter the word or phrase they want in the item properties.

Tags are available from the ribbon **Tag & Notes** button. When clicked, a pop-up opens to allow for tags (including #tags) and notes. Unlike the enterprise keywords, tags are also shown in your My profile page, which can help you find your favorite documents.

Dublin Core

The classic Dublin Core Metadata Element Set is a vocabulary of fifteen metadata elements which can be used in describing documents (or other information assets). The metadata elements are generic by design and they are applicable for a broad range of resources, which is precisely why they pop up in almost any discussion on metadata.

The Dublin Core elements are available as Site Columns in SharePoint. The entire group of fifteen elements is available using the *Dublin Core Columns* content type. A number of columns are also in use as standard columns for document libraries. When your requirements are matched by the Dublin Core columns, you have two options: use the Dublin Core Content type or use your own content type, in which you add a selection of the Dublin Core columns.

The 15 elements of the Dublin Core set are given below. In the list, I combine information from the Dublin Core website (4) with the translation to SharePoint. I had to give the matter some thought, before I was convinced that including the elements in this book provided value to you, as the reader. Ultimately, I decided to do so, because:

- It gives you greater insight into many of the SharePoint standard columns you have been using so long;
- As stated above, Dublin Core tends to pop up in many metadata discussions, so it's good to have an idea of what it is about (as we will see in the next section, there is actually a lot more to Dublin Core then just the fifteen elements presented in the table)
- When you have to describe your own metadata, the definitions from the Dublin Core are an excellent starting point (unless you are working in an environment dominated by academics, I advise you to make the descriptions a little less formal)
- Dublin Core is the basis for almost every metadata standard, both formally and informally. The first category includes ISO Standard 15836:2009 and ANSI/NISO Standard Z39.85-2007
- It can be a checklist to evaluate your own metadata set. This does not mean that you have to include all elements in your metadata scheme, however, see also (5).
- In the descriptions of the elements, guidance is sometimes given on implementation which you can re-use in your SharePoint metadata

- When doing the information analysis, you are likely to come across people with a background in library sciences or archiving. Understanding Dublin Core will help you bridging the communication gap.

Contributor

Definition

An entity responsible for making contributions to the resource.

Comment

Examples of a Contributor include a person, an organization, or a service. Typically, the name of a Contributor should be used to indicate the entity.

SharePoint considerations

The SharePoint *Created by* and *Modified by* columns are available by default in any document library. *Created by*, the author of the initial version of the document, is not made visible in the default view, but *Modified by*, the author of the last version of the document, is. Both are single values, whereas the intention of Dublin Core is to capture all (relevant) contributors. The Contributor column of the Dublin Core columns content type consists of multiple lines of text, which makes it more flexible, but there is also no validation.

Coverage

Definition

The spatial or temporal topic of the resource, the spatial applicability of the resource, or the jurisdiction under which the resource is relevant.

Comment

Spatial topic and spatial applicability may be a named place or a location specified by its geographic coordinates. Temporal topic may be a named period, date, or date range. A jurisdiction may be a named administrative entity or a geographic location to which the resource applies. Recommended best practice is to use a controlled vocabulary such as the Thesaurus of Geographic Names. Where appropriate, named places or time periods can be used in preference to numeric identifiers, such as sets of coordinates or date ranges.

SharePoint considerations

The coverage element is not provided by default. It is very generic, where most use cases benefit from being specific. A generic metadata field such as Coverage would only serve equally generic use cases, such as searching for documents created at a single geographical location. The Coverage column of the Dublin Core columns content type consists of a single line of text.

Creator

Definition

An entity primarily responsible for making the resource.

Comment

Examples of a Creator include a person, an organization, or a service. Typically, the name of a Creator should be used to indicate the entity.

SharePoint considerations

The SharePoint *Created by* column is available by default in any document library and has the same meaning as the Dublin Core creator field. It is not made visible in the default view. Related fields are *Modified by* and *Created* (refer to Contributor and date in this table, respectively). The Creator column of the Dublin Core columns content type consists of a single line of text.

Date

Definition

A point or period of time associated with an event in the lifecycle of the resource.

Comment

Date may be used to express temporal information at any level of granularity. Recommended best practice is to use an encoding scheme, such as the W3CDTF profile of ISO 8601.

SharePoint considerations

The SharePoint *Created* and *Modified* columns are available by default in any document library. *Created*, the date of initial creation of the document is not made visible in the default view, but modified, the last date the document was *Modified*, is. Both are single values, whereas the intention of Dublin Core is to capture all (relevant) dates. The Dublin Core columns content type contains the Date Created and Data modified columns of type Date. Having Date types seems out of synch with having free format fields for contributor and creator.

Description

Definition

An account of the resource.

Comment

Description may include but is not limited to: an abstract, a table of contents, a graphical representation, or a free-text account of the resource.

| *SharePoint considerations* | The description element is not included by default. Think carefully about whether this field is required. A combination of title and keywords may be enough for your purpose especially in combination with the standard text search capabilities within SharePoint. The Description column of the Dublin Core columns content type contains multiple lines of text. |

Format

| *Definition* | The file format, physical medium, or dimensions of the resource. |

| *Comment* | Examples of dimensions include size and duration. Recommended best practice is to use a controlled vocabulary such as the list of Internet Media Types. |

| *SharePoint considerations* | The Format column is not included by default. SharePoint does provide the File size column, which provides information in addition to the type. This is in line with the examples given by Dublin Core in (6).The Format column of the Dublin Core columns content type consists of a single line of text, which makes it more flexible, but there is also no validation. |

Identifier

| *Definition* | An unambiguous reference to the resource within a given context. |

| *Comment* | Recommended best practice is to identify the resource by means of a string conforming to a formal identification system. |

| *SharePoint considerations* | The SharePoint ID column is available by default in any document library. This is not a universal ID however, suitable to match the intention of the Identifier column. It is simply a number starting from 1, within each document library. The Document ID feature does provide functionality in line with the Dublin Core Identifier element. Before using the Document ID feature in your content management system, you must first enable it for the site collection(s) in which your documents are hosted. When the service is enabled, a new column is automatically added to the Document and Document Set content types. The Resource Identifier column of the Dublin Core columns content type consists of a single line of text, which makes it |

more flexible to use your own formats, but the benefits of using the Document ID feature are also missing (Unique ID, link to document is stable, even after moving the document).

Language

Definition

A language of the resource.

Comment

Recommended best practice is to use a controlled vocabulary such as RFC 4646.

SharePoint considerations

The Language column is not available by default in a document library. The Language column of the Dublin Core columns content type is of the Choice type. It provides a list of choices that will be workable in most situations, but it is not RFC 4646-compliant.

Publisher

Definition

An entity responsible for making the resource available.

Comment

Examples of a Publisher include a person, an organization, or a service. Typically, the name of a Publisher should be used to indicate the entity.

SharePoint considerations

The Publisher column is not available by default in a document library. The purpose of this field is to identify the entity that provides access to it. Within SharePoint, this may be the creator as specified in the Created By column. In many cases it will be an organizational unit. The concept is related to ownership as often encountered in SharePoint solutions. The owner is not only responsible for rights to the document, but also for the quality of the document. In some cases an Owner column is useful, and in other cases ownership is determined at a higher level (typically site or site collection). The Publisher column of the Dublin Core columns content type consists of a single line of text.

Relation

Definition

A related resource.

Comment

Recommended best practice is to identify the related resource by means of a string conforming to a formal identification system.

SharePoint considerations	The Relation column is not available by default in a document library. Relationship as meant within Dublin Core is very generic. More useful in the SharePoint context would be referring to other documents either via Document ID or with links. Using document sets would also be a way to relate documents to one another. The Relation column of the Dublin Core columns content type contains multiple lines of text.

Rights

Definition	Information about rights held in and over the resource.
Comment	Typically, rights information includes a statement about various property rights associated with the resource, including intellectual property rights.
SharePoint considerations	The Rights column is not available by default in a document library. Note this is something different to the access rights. The Rights Management column of the Dublin Core columns content type contains multiple lines of text.

Source

Definition	A related resource from which the described resource is derived.
Comment	The described resource may be derived from the related resource in whole or in part. Recommended best practice is to identify the related resource by means of a string conforming to a formal identification system.
SharePoint considerations	The Source column is not available by default in a document library. Source may be regarded as a subset of Relation. Evaluate whether you really have a need to use a separate column for Source. The Source column of the Dublin Core columns content type contains multiple lines of text.

Subject

Definition	The topic of the resource.
Comment	Typically, the subject will be represented using keywords, key phrases, or classification codes. Recommended best practice is to use a controlled vocabulary.

SharePoint considerations	The Subject column is not available by default in a document library. For SharePoint, the best conceivable general implementation would be to use Enterprise Keywords, see the section *Tagging & Enterprise keywords*, in this chapter. Note that these are *general* keywords. In most cases you will need specific metadata as well. The Subject column of the Dublin Core columns content type consists of a single line of text. It also contains the Keywords column, containing multiple lines of text. It seems Microsoft added its own flavor by separating Subject and Keywords.

Title

Definition	A name given to the resource.
Comment	Typically, a Title will be a name by which the resource is formally known.
SharePoint considerations	The SharePoint Title column is available by default in any document library. It is not made visible in the default view. SharePoint also has two Name columns, which refer to the file name and which are automatically updated when uploading or saving. One of the Name columns has the Document Edit context menu attached to it, so in most cases, you will need it. The Title column of the Dublin Core columns content type consists of a single line of text. Since there are also standard Title and Name columns, it seems superfluous.

Type

Definition	The nature or genre of the resource.
Comment	Recommended best practice is to use a controlled vocabulary such as the DCMI Type Vocabulary. To describe the file format, physical medium, or dimensions of the resource, use the Format element.
SharePoint considerations	The SharePoint Type column is available by default in any document library. It is also one of four columns that is visible in the default view. Since only files can live within SharePoint, the type is always a file type. These file types do not match the DCMI Type Vocabulary. In all but some very generic cases, the file type will be of more value to future users then the DCMI Type. The type is made visible by a pictogram. The Resource Type column of the Dublin Core columns content type

consists of a single line of text. It is more flexible then the default type column, but also it does not have its advantages, such as being determined automatically and being shown by a symbol easily recognized by the majority of users.

Dublin Core provides creators and dates as singular elements, whereas in most cases, you want to see what where the contributions of creators on specific date. So there is a triad contributor – contribution – date. SharePoint provides this metadata in the version history (when switched on) in conjunction with the change history in Word (when switched on). In this way you have a much more detailed account of what happened historically with the document then metadata fields could provide. Also, metadata such as this is commonly put in the version history in the document itself. In some cases (such as eDiscovery), you would may have a need to search for a specific date or contributor without knowing which document to search. Targeted metadata such as the Dublin Core columns Date and Creator are then ideal. SharePoint standard search might help you as well, but the name of the creator is then not targeted as a creator-name and the date is not targeted as a specific creation-date. If you know which document you want to search for a specific date or creator (which is commonly the case) then the mechanisms above are sufficient. Be aware that standard search can still find the creators and dates if they are mentioned in the version history or some other place in the document. The message here is to keep the metadata use cases in mind before you start introducing new metadata fields, but this is of course true for any metadata field. It is also possible to incorporate the SharePoint version in a Word document, similar to the one described in the section *Template based transfer*.

Since the version is a system column however, you cannot use the Quick Parts in the simple way, but you have to use SharePoint labels to transfer the values to Word.

When using SharePoint standard columns for an entity with another name in the Dublin Core set, you must verify that no problems arise as a consequence. When you are keeping records up to 10 years, to then be destroyed, this will probably not be the case if you have documented your decision in the information architecture or some other place. When your records are meant to be kept 'eternally', such as documents with historical value, this might not be the case. You may need to use the Dublin Core columns or, alternatively, rename the columns when the records are transferred to the central archive.

Dublin Core qualifiers

In the previous section we saw the basic elements of Dublin Core (the Simple level). The model can be extended by using qualifiers (the Qualified level), which provide additional meaning to the metadata value:

- Element Refinement. These qualifiers make the meaning of an element narrower or more specific. A refined element shares the meaning of the unqualified element, but with a more restricted scope. A client that does not understand a specific element refinement term should be able to ignore the qualifier and treat the metadata value as if it were an unqualified (broader) element. The definitions of element refinement terms for qualifiers must be publicly available.
- Encoding Scheme. These qualifiers identify schemes that aid the interpretation of an element value. These schemes include controlled vocabularies and formal notations or parsing rules. A value expressed using an encoding scheme will thus be a token selected from a controlled vocabulary (e.g., a term from a classification system or set of subject headings) or a string formatted in accordance with a formal notation (e.g., "2000-01-01" as the standard expression of a date). If an encoding scheme is not understood by a client or agent, the value may still be useful to a human reader. The definitive description of an encoding scheme for qualifiers must be clearly identified and available for public use.

A full list of all qualifiers can be found on the Dublin Core site (7). Note that this approach is valuable only if you need to adhere to the Dublin Core metadata elements. In this case, the qualifiers do provide you the opportunity to give extra information on the metadata. In most cases within the SharePoint context, you will be better off using a more specific metadata field name. So instead of specifying a date and then qualifying it as a creation date, use the default Created metadata column.

Dublin Core Application Profiles (DCAP)

When your organization has specific metadata, yet wishes to base this as far as possible on existing standards, consider a DCAP. This will be the case if the records are assumed to have longevity and a broad audience. This means that no knowledge can be assumed on the interpretation and encoding of the metadata. Another advantage is that metadata can be machine-processed more easily.

A DCAP is a document (or set of documents) that specifies and describes the metadata used in a particular application. To accomplish this, such a profile:

- describes what a community wants to accomplish with its application (Functional Requirements);
- characterizes the types of things described by the metadata and their relationships (Domain Model);
- enumerates the metadata terms to be used and the rules for their use (Description Set Profile and Usage Guidelines); and
- defines the machine syntax that will be used to encode the data (Syntax Guidelines and Data Formats).

At this point I am not interested so much in the horizontal ordering, as requirements elicitation and machine encoding are out of the scope of this book. It is useful to include some words on the vertical ordering, however, because this is a general principle that might well be applied in SharePoint environments.

A DCAP identifies the source of metadata terms used — whether they have been defined in formally maintained standards such as Dublin Core, in less formally defined element sets and vocabularies, or by the creator of the DCAP itself for local use in an application. Optionally, a DCAP may provide additional documentation on how the terms are constrained, encoded or interpreted for application-specific purposes (9).

A graphical representation of the DCAP is provided in Figure 8.8. The lighter blocks are described in the next paragraphs.

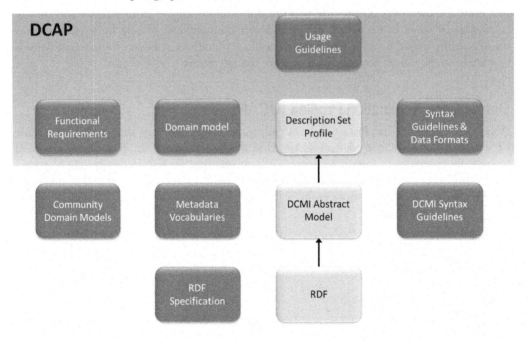

Figure 8.8: DCAP

Description Set Profile

A Description Set is a set of statements about a resource. It basically consists of property-value pairs, for example the *Author* metadata property of the "A345 Biochem" manual, having the value *Kate Blunsdon*. A Description Set groups Descriptions into the full set for a resource. For example, the manual "A345 Biochem" has the following Description Set:

- Name: A345 Biochem
- Author: Kate Blunsdon
- Created: 2-3-2010
- Category: Biochemical
- Etc.

See the website of Dublin Core (4) for more formal treatment.

Not all combinations of properties and values will make sense. A manual can have multiple authors, but will always have a single name. Created is a date, so the value should be a valid date. The category will be one of a limited set of options. These rules are formalized in a DSP, a Description Set Profile. An XML Schema (xsd) is well suited to do just that. Note that a DSP just constrains the syntactic aspects of the elements. Usage guidelines will need to be supplied in order to deal with semantic aspects that could range from demanding a certain format for the name, the fact that only biochemical engineers can be the author of a Biochemical manual, to checking that the creation date matches with some other dates. More information on Description Set Templates can be found at the website of Dublin Core (6).

To give you an I idea, I have added an example in Figure 8.9. As you can see, the DSP is very specific, so each new domain requires its own DSP.

```xml
<?xml version="1.0" encoding="UTF-8"?>
<DescriptionSetTemplate xmlns="http://dublincore.org/xml/dc-dsp/2008/01/14"
    xmlns:xsi="http://www.w3.org/2001/XMLSchema-instance"
    xsi:schemaLocation="http://dublincore.org/xml/dc-dsp/2008/01/14">
    <DescriptionTemplate ID="Book" minOccurs="1" maxOccurs="1" standalone="yes">
        <StatementTemplate ID="title" minOccurs="1" maxOccurs="1" type="literal">
            <Property>http://purl.org/dc/terms/title</Property>
        </StatementTemplate>
        <StatementTemplate ID="dateCreated" minOccurs="0" maxOccurs="1" type="literal">
            <Property>http://purl.org/dc/terms/created</Property>
            <LiteralConstraint>
                <SyntaxEncodingScheme>http://purl.org/dc/terms/W3CDTF</SyntaxEncodingScheme>
            </LiteralConstraint>
        </StatementTemplate>
        <StatementTemplate ID="language" minOccurs="0" maxOccurs="3" type="nonliteral">
            <Property>http://purl.org/dc/terms/language</Property>
            <NonLiteralConstraint>
                <VocabularyEncodingSchemeURI>http://purl.org/dc/terms/ISO639-3</VocabularyEncodingSchemeURI>
                <ValueStringConstraint minOccurs="1" maxOccurs="1"/>
            </NonLiteralConstraint>
        </StatementTemplate>
        <StatementTemplate ID="subject" minOccurs="0" maxOccurs="infinite" type="nonliteral">
            <Property>http://purl.org/dc/terms/LCSH</Property>
            <NonLiteralConstraint>
                <VocabularyEncodingSchemeURI>http://lcsh.info</VocabularyEncodingSchemeURI>
                <ValueStringConstraint minOccurs="1" maxOccurs="1"/>
            </NonLiteralConstraint>
        </StatementTemplate>
        <StatementTemplate ID="author" minOccurs="0" maxOccurs="5" type="nonliteral">
            <Property>http://purl.org/dc/terms/creator</Property>
            <NonLiteralConstraint descriptionTemplateRef="person"/>
        </StatementTemplate>
    </DescriptionTemplate>
    <DescriptionTemplate ID="person" minOccurs="0"  standalone="no">
```

```
<StatementTemplate ID="givenName" minOccurs="0" maxOccurs="1" type="literal">
    <Property>http://xmlns.com/foaf/0.1/givenname</Property>
</StatementTemplate>
<StatementTemplate ID="familyName" minOccurs="0" maxOccurs="1" type="literal">
    <Property>http://xmlns.com/foaf/0.1/family_name</Property>
</StatementTemplate>
<StatementTemplate ID="email" minOccurs="0"  type="nonliteral">
    <Property>http://xmlns.com/foaf/0.1/mbox</Property>
    <NonLiteralConstraint>
        <ValueURIOccurrence>mandatory</ValueURIOccurrence>
    </NonLiteralConstraint>
</StatementTemplate>
    </DescriptionTemplate>
</DescriptionSetTemplate>
```

Figure 8.9: DSP example (10)

DCAM (DCMI Abstract Model)

The DCAM provides the underlying rules for DSPs. This allows for DSPs to be read and to a certain extent, interpreted by computer programs. It also ensures interoperability between applications. When you are storing records in such a way that you cannot make assumptions about the reader or the time of use, it makes sense to use a scheme based on DCAM. It is also why this is relevant in some SharePoint scenarios as many governmental agencies have metadata schemes based on DCAM. Records may be stored as part of the cultural heritance, for example, as is the case in the Netherlands where all governmental agencies are required to contribute, if applicable. The DCAM consists of the Resource Model, the Description Set Model and the Vocabulary Model. To put it simply, they describe how a resource (for instance, a document) can have descriptions consisting of statements, which in turn consist of property-value pairs. Interestingly, a record within DCMI is defined as "record is some structured metadata about a resource, comprising one or more properties and their associated values". This is different to how most people define a record, namely as an item of information or more formally "information created, received, and maintained as evidence and information by an organization or person, in pursuance of legal obligations or in the transaction of business" (1). DCMI tries to combine the 'web world' (see the section on RDF) with the records management world. In some cases, this leads to difficult decisions.

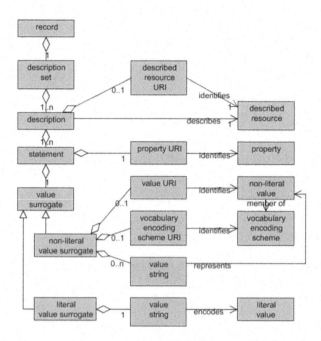

Figure 8.10: The Description Set Model of DCAM (8)

To give you an idea of DCAM, I have included the Description Set Model in Figure 8.10. There is only one DCAM, which is the basis for many DSPs.

RDF

The Resource Description Framework RDF is not 'owned' by DCMI, but it is a standard of W3C. If you really want to understand DCAM, it is best to start by studying the RDF. A good reference for this is the RDF primer of W3C (11). The RDF is used to represent information about resources on the World Wide Web by providing elements such as those we see in SharePoint or Dublin Core. Examples include title, author, creation date, modification date etc. The resources described by using RDF are not limited to information resources such as pages, documents and images, but can also include entities such as items available from online shopping.

Like DCAM, RDF is intended for processing by computer programs, and an important aspect is to realize interoperability by providing a common framework.

The DCAM use of Uniform Resource Identifiers (URIs) is also based on RDF. The idea is to describe resources with so called statements based on properties and property values. Like DCAM, the RDF is generic.

References

1. ISO 15489-1. Information and documentation – records management –part 1: general

2. ISO 23081: Information and documentation - Records management processes - Metadata for records

3. ISO Technical Committee (TC) 46, Subcommittee (SC) 11. N800R1: Where to start advice on creating a metadata schema

4. http://dublincore.org/

5. http://dublincore.org/documents/dcmi-type-vocabulary/

6. http://dublincore.org/documents/usageguide/elements.shtml

7. http://dublincore.org/documents/usageguide/qualifiers.shtml

8. http://dublincore.org/documents/abstract-model/

9. CWA 14855:2003: Dublin Core application profile guidelines

10. http://dublincore.org/documents/profile-guidelines/index.shtml

11. http://www.w3.org/TR/2004/REC-rdf-primer-20040210/

Index

CPSIA information can be obtained
at www.ICGtesting.com
Printed in the USA
LVOW06s1343230917
549813LV00003B/146/P